cute & easy
crochet

cute & easy
crochet

Learn to crochet with these 35 adorable projects

Nicki Trench

CICO BOOKS
LONDON NEW YORK

Published in 2011 by CICO Books
an imprint of Ryland Peters & Small Ltd
519 Broadway, 5th Floor, New York, NY 10012

www.cicobooks.com

20 19 18 17 16 15 14 13 12 11 10

ISBN 978 1 907563 20 1

Printed in China

Editor: Marie Clayton
Designer: Christine Wood
Photographer: Penny Wincer
Stylist: Alison Davidson. Additional styling by
Rose Hammick.

Contents

Introduction

I'm delighted by the latest enthusiasm for crochet and *Cute & Easy Crochet* aims to inspire and meet with current trends to entice and feed all levels with great patterns and designs.

Modern colors and yarns have transformed crochet and shaken off any negative reputation. The granny square has emerged with glorious colors and luxurious crochet pieces have swamped the high streets with pretty scarves, cool dresses, and elegant wraps.

Crochet has now established itself as a popular contemporary craft with people flocking to classes to learn this traditional skill that has somehow missed a generation, while the previous generations took it for granted as a handed-down knowledge.

In *Cute & Easy Crochet*, we've divided the projects into chapters that cover the various skill groups: Starting Out for the Beginner, Practice Makes Perfect for Improvers and Confident Crocheting for Enthusiasts. We've used up-to-date yarns and simple designs that will inspire you whatever your level; there is something in *Cute & Easy Crochet* for all. Beginners will love the easy projects in Starting Out that need only the basic skills and stitches; see the gorgeous Rose Shopper (page 40), the Round Stripy Pillow Cover (page 32), or try the stunning Springtime Throw made of lots of little easy squares (page 24).

Once you've gathered confidence, the Practice Makes Perfect projects start to introduce edgings and a little more intricate pattern reading, while still keeping things simple. See the Chunky Seashell Scarf (page 68) or the coziest gloves you've ever seen (page 74).

The Confident Crochet section is for those enthusiasts who are very comfortable reading patterns and have mastered and practiced the basic techniques. You won't be able to resist the Babushkas (page 96), the Summer Evening Shawl (page 112), or the blanket made with my favorite squares: Camellia Blanket (page 88).

If you're making for a baby, we have some lovely designs and easy projects: Baby Blanket (page 66), Baby Slippers (page 84), and the delightful teddies, Monty and Priscilla (page 120). If you'd like to make an original gift, try the brilliant Baby Bibs (page 82).

Cute & Easy Crochet has an excellent Crochet Know-how section with clear illustrations that will show you exactly how to master the techniques used in the patterns. Don't be put off by crochet abbreviations, they are really easy to master and explained in each pattern.

As soon as I was commissioned to write this book, I immediately rushed to my local haberdashery and bought ribbons and trimmings to use as my color palette guide. I hope the light blues, yellows, pinks, greens, and lilacs will evoke the atmosphere of spring and summer, even if you're crocheting in the middle of winter in front of the fire.

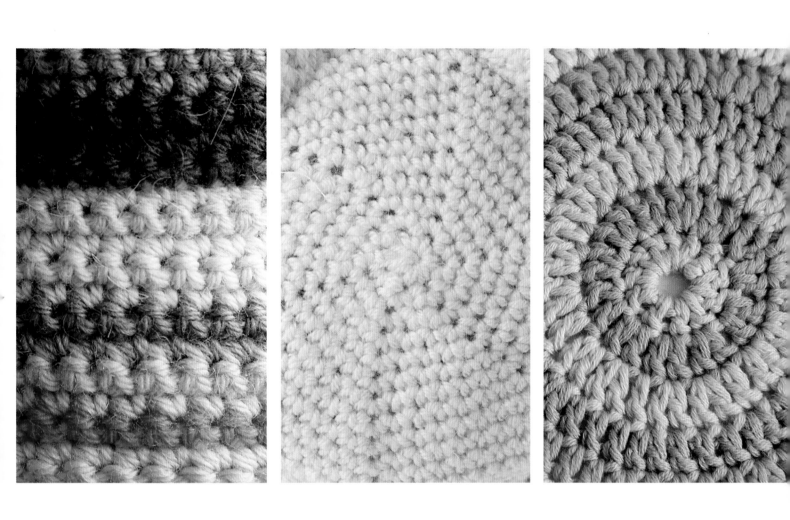

Crochet know-how

Techniques

In this section, we explain how to master the simple crochet techniques that you need to make the projects in this book.

Making a slip knot

The simplest way is to make a circle with the yarn, so that the loop is facing downwards.

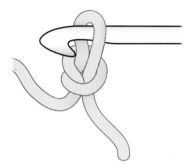

1 In one hand, hold the circle at the top, where the yarn crosses, and let the tail drop down so that it falls in the center of the loop. With your free hand, or the tip of the crochet hook, pull the tail through the loop and pull the knot so that it tightens loosely.

2 Put the hook into the circle and pull the knot gently so that it forms a loose loop on the hook.

Holding the hook

Pick up your hook as though you were picking up a pen or pencil. Keeping the hook held loosely between your fingers and thumb, turn your hand so that the palm is facing up and the hook is balanced in your hand and resting in the space between your index finger and your thumb.

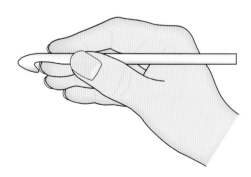

Holding yarn

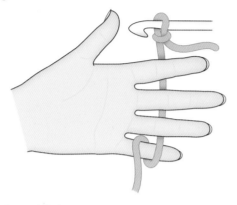

Pick up the yarn with your little finger in the opposite hand to your hook, with your palm facing upwards. Turn your hand to face downwards, with the yarn on top of your index finger and under the other two fingers and wrapped right around the little finger. Keeping your index finger only at a slight curve, hold your work just under the slip knot with the other hand.

Yarn over hook

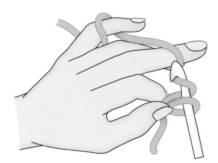

To create a stitch, you'll need to catch the yarn with the hook and pull it through the loop. Holding your yarn and hook correctly, catch the yarn from behind with the hook pointed upwards. As you gently pull the yarn through the loop on the hook, turn the hook so that it faces downwards and slide the yarn through the loop. The loop on the hook should be kept loose enough so that the hook slides through easily.

Chain

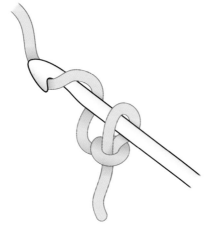

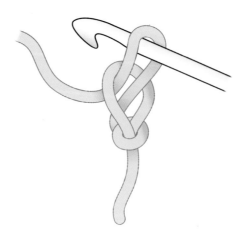

1 Using the hook, wrap the yarn round the hook and pull it through the loop on the hook, creating a new loop on the hook. Continue in this way to create a chain of the required length.

2 Keep moving your middle finger and thumb close to the hook, to hold the work in place with the opposite hand that you hold your hook with.

Chain ring/circle

If you are crocheting a round shape, one way of starting off is by crocheting a number of chains following the instructions in your pattern, and then joining them into a circle.

1 To join the chain into a circle, insert the crochet hook into the first chain that you made (not into the slip knot), yarn over hook, then pull the yarn through the chain and through the loop on your hook at the same time, thereby creating a slip stitch and forming a circle.

2 You will now have a circle ready according to your pattern.

Some of the circles in this book have been made by creating a spiral, whereby you make two chains and insert your hook into the second chain from the hook (the first chain you made). Following the instructions in the pattern will then ensure the spiral has the correct amount of stitches. It's essential to use a stitch marker when using this method, so that you know where to start and finish your round.

Chain space

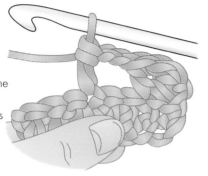

1 A chain space (ch sp) is the space that has been made under a chain in the previous round or row and falls in between other stitches.

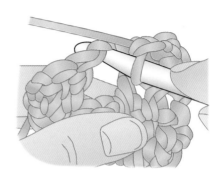

2 Stitches into a chain space are made directly into the hole created under the chain and not into the chain stitches themselves.

Marking rounds

Place a stitch marker at the beginning of each round; a piece of yarn in a contrasting color is useful for this. Loop the stitch marker into the first stitch. When you have made a round and reached the point where the stitch marker is, work this stitch, take out the stitch marker from the previous round and put it back into the first stitch of the new round.

Slip stitch

A slip stitch doesn't create any height and is often used as the last stitch to create a smooth and even round or row.

1 To make a slip stitch: put the hook through the work, yarn over hook.

2 Pull the yarn through both the work and through the loop on the hook at the same time.

Single crochet

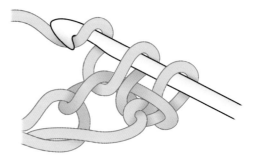

1 Insert the hook into your work, yarn over hook and pull the yarn through the work. You will then have two loops on the hook.

2 Yarn over hook again and pull through the two loops on the hook. You will then have one loop on the hook.

Half double

1 Before inserting the hook into the work, wrap the yarn around the hook and put the hook through the work with the yarn wrapped around.

2 Yarn over hook again and pull through the first loop on the hook (you now have three loops on the hook).

3 Yarn over hook and pull the yarn through all three loops. You'll be left with one loop on the hook.

Double crochet

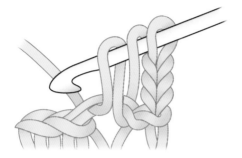

1 Before inserting the hook into the work, wrap the yarn around the hook and put the hook through the work with the yarn wrapped around.

2 Yarn over hook again and pull through the first loop on the hook (you now have three loops on the hook). yarn over hook again, pull the yarn through two loops (you now have two loops on the hook).

3 Pull the yarn through two loops again. You will be left with one loop on the hook.

Treble crochet

Yarn round hook twice, insert hook into the stitch, yarn round hook, pull a loop through (four loops on hook), yarn round hook, pull the yarn through two stitches (three loops on hook), yarn round hook, pull a loop through the next two stitches (two loops on hook), yarn round hook, pull a loop through the last two stitches.

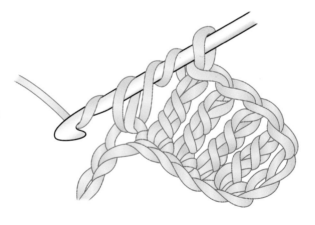

Double treble crochet

Yarn round hook three times, insert hook into the stitch, yarn round hook, pull a loop through (five loops on hook), yarn round hook, pull the yarn through two stitches (four loops on hook), yarn round hook, pull a loop through the next two stitches (three loops on hook), yarn round hook, pull a loop through the next two stitches (two loops on hook), yarn round hook, pull a loop hrough the last two stitches.

Making rows

When making straight rows, you need to make a turning chain at the end to create the height you need for the stitch you're working with. To do this you just make the right number of chains for the stitch you are working in as follows:

Single crochet = 1 chain
Half double crochet = 2 chain
Double crochet = 3 chain
Treble crochet = 4 chain

Joining new yarn

If using single crochet, insert the hook as normal into the stitch, using the original yarn, and pull a loop through. Drop the old yarn and pick up the new yarn. Wrap the new yarn round the hook and pull it through the two loops on the hook.

Decreasing

You can decease by either missing the next stitch and continuing to crochet, or by crocheting two or more stitches together. The basic technique is the same no matter which stitch you are using; the illustration shows working three doubles (dc3tog) in progress:

Work a double crochet into each of the next three stitches as normal, but leave the last loop of each stitch on the hook (four loops on the hook). Yarn over hook and pull the yarn through all the stitches on the hook to join them together. You will finish with one loop on the hook.

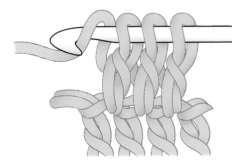

Increasing

Make two or three stitches into one stitch from the previous row. The illustration shows a two-stitch increase being made.

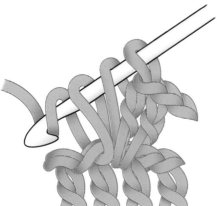

Single crochet two stitches together

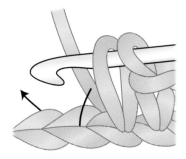

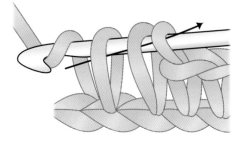

1 Insert hook into next stitch, draw a loop through, insert hook into next stitch.

2 Draw a loop through, yarn round hook andd pull through all three stitches.

Half double two stitches together

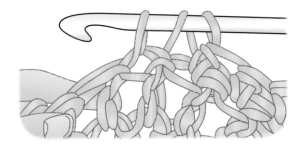

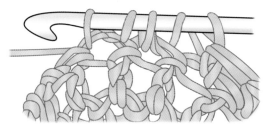

1 Yarn round hook, insert hook into next stitch, yarn round hook, draw yarn through (three loops on hook).

2 Yarn round hook, insert hook into next stitch, yarn round hook, draw yarn through.

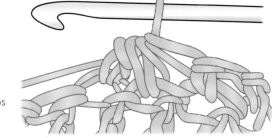

3 Draw yarn through all five loops on hook.

How to single crochet squares together

Place two squares wrong sides together, lining them up so that the stitches on each square match. Put the hook through the top loops of the first square and also through the corresponding top loops of the second square. Join in the yarn, make 1 chain, insert the hook into the top stitches of both squares, and make a single crochet seam across the top of the squares.

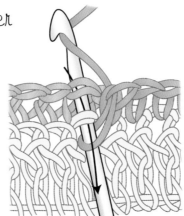

Cluster

Yarn round hook, insert hook into next stitch, pull yarn through work, yarn round hook, insert hook into same stitch, pull yarn through work, yarn round hook, insert hook into same stitch, pull yarn through work. Pull yarn through all seven loops on hook, 1 chain.

Fastening off

Cut the yarn leaving a tail of approx 4in (10cm). Pull the tail all the way through the loop.

chapter 1

Starting out

Springtime Throw

This is a delightful project and the squares are very easy and perfect for a beginner. It's the colors of the Rooster yarn that make this so special—but it also works well using scraps of yarn.

level 1: Beginner

materials
Rooster Almerino light worsted/DK (50% baby alpaca, 50% merino wool)
21 x 50g balls (2604yds/2362.5m) 201 Cornish (MC)
5 x 50g balls (620yds/562.5m) each of:
209 Smoothie
207 Gooseberry
203 Strawberry Cream
205 Glace
204 Grape
210 Custard
F/5 (4mm) crochet hook

abbreviations
ch chain
ch sp chain space
dc double crochet
rep repeat
sc single crochet
ss slip stitch
st(s) stitch(es)
WS wrong side

finished measurement
Approx. 64 x 88in. (162 x 223cm)

gauge
Gauge is not critical on this project.

method

Make 432 squares in total: 14 each of 30 different color combinations (420 squares), plus another 12 random colorways. On every square, Round 2 is made using MC.

square

Using first color, make a loop, then make 4ch. Join with ss into first ch to form a ring.

Round 1: 3ch, 2dc into ring, 2ch, 3dc into ring, 2ch, *3dc into ring, 2ch; rep from * once more.

Ss into top of first 3ch.

Fasten off.

Place hook through a ch sp and join in MC.

Round 2: 3ch, 2dc, 3ch, 3dc into same ch sp (first corner), 2ch, *3dc, 3ch, 3dc into next ch sp, 2ch; rep from * twice more.

Ss into top of first 3ch.

Fasten off.

Put hook into top of fastened-off stitch, join in third color, make 1ch.

Round 3: 1sc into top of next 2 sts, 3sc into next ch sp, 1sc into top of next 3 sts, 2sc into next ch sp, *1sc into top of next 3 sts, 3sc into next ch sp, 1sc into top of next 3 sts, 2sc into next ch sp; rep from * twice more.

Ss into top of first ch.

Fasten off.

Sew in ends neatly and securely after making each square.

to make up

Lay out the squares with 18 squares across (width) by 24 squares down (length) in a random order. Using MC and with WS together, join squares first in horizontal rows and then in vertical rows, using a sc seam. When all squares are joined, work one row of sc edging all the way around blanket. When turning corners, make 2sc, 1ch, 2sc into each corner stitch.

Fasten off.

Sew in ends.

---

tip

This is a large blanket and takes up a lot of balls of yarn. It's made up from lots of small squares, so it's very easy to adjust the sizing by making fewer or more squares; just remember to adjust the yarn quantities.

Knickerbockerglory Bunting

Bunting evokes all the atmosphere of spring and summer, whatever the weather and wherever you hang it. It's a lovely, happy way to brighten up a child's room, a yard, a kitchen, a hallway, or just about anywhere at all.

level 1: Beginner

materials

King Cole Merino Blend light worsted/DK (100% merino wool)
1 x 50g ball (123yds/112m) each of:
5 Sky
55 Gold
94 Dusky Pink
787 Fuchsia
Debbie Bliss Cashmerino light worsted/DK (55% merino wool, 33% microfibre, 12% cashmere)
1 x 50g ball (120yds/110m) each of:
017 Lilac
029 Light green
Rowan Belle Organic light worsted/DK (50% organic wool, 50% cotton)
1 x 50g ball (131yds/120m) 004 Persimmon
F/5 (4mm) crochet hook
Wool/tapestry needle

abbreviations

ch chain
dc double crochet
rep repeat
RS right side
sc single crochet
sc2tog Insert hook into next st, draw a loop through, insert hook into next st, draw a loop through, pull through all 3 sts.
ss slip stitch
st(s) stitch(es)

finished measurement
Each flag approx. 7in. (18cm) across top

gauge
Gauge is not critical on this project.

method
Make 6, or as many as required, in different colors with contrast edgings.
flag
Using flag main color, make 26ch.
Row 1: 1sc in 2nd ch from hook, 1sc in each ch to end. (25 sts)
Row 2: 1ch, sc2tog, 1sc in each st to end.
Rep Row 2 until 2 sts remain, sc2tog.
Fasten off.

edging
With RS facing, join in first contrast color into top right corner st, 3ch, make 24dc along top edge.
Fasten off.

With RS facing, join next contrast color in top left corner, 1ch, work 26sc along first side, 3sc in corner st, 26sc along other side, ending with a ss into top of first double.
Fasten off.
Sew in ends.

to make up
With contrasting col, make 70ch. With RS facing, join ch to first flag with ss in right-hand corner, 1ch, *1sc in between each dc across top of flag to end. Join next flag with ss into top right-hand corner; rep from * to end for each flag, ss into last corner st of last flag. Make 70ch. Fasten off.

Using a wool/tapestry needle at back of work, stitch to secure joins in between each flag, using loose ends of wool. Sew in ends well. Press each flag.

> **tips**
> If you'd like to stiffen your flags, try using a little starch before hanging.
>
> Making bunting out of your odds and ends of yarn is ideal and a great way to use up spare yarn left over from other projects.
>
> I have chosen colors from different brands to get the yummy color scheme—just make sure that the yarn is a similar weight.

Hook Holder

This is such a handy little tool kit and great for keeping your crochet hooks in. The spacing instructions here give you room for 12 hooks; just sew more lines into the lining for more hook spaces.

level 1: Beginner

materials

Rooster Almerino light worsted/DK (50% baby alpaca, 50% merino wool)
1 x 50g ball (124yds/112.5m) each of:
210 Custard (A)
204 Grape (B)
F/5 (4mm) crochet hook
9 x 13in. (23 x 33cm) fabric for main lining
7 x 13in. (18 x 33cm) fabric for pockets
39in. (1m) x ⅝in. (1.5cm) wide ribbon
Sewing needle and thread

abbreviations

ch chain
rep repeat
RS right side
sc single crochet
ss slip stitch
st(s) stitch(es)
WS wrong side

finished measurement

11½ x 8in. (29 x 20cm)

gauge

Gauge is not critical on this project.

method

Using A, make 33ch.
Row 1: 1sc in next ch from hook and in every ch to end. (32 sts)
Rep Row 1 until work measures 11½in. (29cm).
Fasten off.

edging

With RS facing and using B, make 58sc along one long edge, turn.
Next row: 1sc into first st, *3ch, ss into third ch from hook, skip 1 st, 1sc; rep from * to * to end.
Fasten off.
Rep on opposite long edge.
Fasten off.
Block and steam work.
When working on the main crochet piece from here on, the longest side becomes the width of the hook roll holder and the shorter side becomes the height.

lining

Measure crochet piece, adding ⅝in. (1.5cm) to each side for hem allowances, and cut main lining fabric to size. Pin and press under a ⅝in. (1.5cm) hem to the WS on each side, and machine stitch. Sew top edge hem using a zigzag stitch.

Cut the pocket lining piece to the same width, but 3in. (7.5cm) shorter. Pin and press under a ⅝in. (1.5cm) hem to the WS on all edges.

With RS of both pieces facing upward, pin pocket lining to main lining, matching bottom edges and leaving an approx 3in (7.5cm) gap at the top. Sew pocket lining to main lining along the two short sides and the bottom edge, leaving the top open. To create the hook pockets, sew vertical lines down the pocket lining at approx 1in (2.5cm) intervals. Pin the whole lining piece to the wrong side of the crochet piece. Cut ribbon length in half. Insert approx 1in (2.5cm) of one ribbon piece halfway down the left-hand side, between the lining and main crochet piece.

to make up

With WS together, hand stitch the lining onto the crochet piece, incorporating the end of the ribbon. Starting from the short side opposite the ribbon, roll up the case. Pin and sew the other ribbon end onto hook piece to correspond with first ribbon end.

Floral Purse

This is a really easy and pretty purse to make and a great beginner's project, which takes only a small amount of time to achieve maximum effect.

level 1: Beginner

materials

Debbie Bliss Cashmerino worsted/Aran (55% merino wool, 33% microfibre, 12% cashmere)
1 x 50g ball (98yds/90m) 011 Green (MC)
Small lengths of light worsted/DK yarn in pinks, purples, blues, and yellow for flowers
G/6 (4.5mm) and F/5 (4mm) crochet hooks
Yarn sewing needle
10 x 12in. (25.5 x 30.5cm) piece of lining fabric
Sewing needle and thread
1 x ½in. (1cm) button

abbreviations

ch chain
ch sp chain space
dc double crochet
hdc half double
rep repeat
RS right side
sc single crochet
ss slip stitch
st(s) stitch(es)
WS wrong side

special abbreviations

hdc2tog Yarn over hook, insert hook into next st, yarn over hook, draw a loop through, insert hook into next st, draw a loop through, yarn over hook and pull through all 4 loops.

finished measurement

Approx. 6 x 4in. (15 x 10cm)

gauge

Gauge is not critical on this project.

method

Using MC and G/6 (4.5mm) hook, make 24ch.
Row 1: 1hdc into second ch from hook, 1hdc in each ch to end, 2ch, turn. (22 sts–2ch counts as first hdc)
Row 2: 1hdc into each st, 2ch, turn.
Rep Row 2 until work measures approx. 7½in. (19cm).

Make flap:
Rows 1–4: 2ch, hdc2tog, 1hdc in each st to end. (18 sts)
Rows 5–7: 2ch, hdc2tog, 1hdc to last 2 sts, hdc2tog. (12 sts)

Make buttonhole:
Row 1: 2ch, hdc2tog, 1hdc in each of next 2 sts, 2ch, skip 2 sts, 1hdc in each of next 3 sts, hdc2tog.
Row 2: 2ch, hdc2tog, 1hdc in next st, 2hdc in ch sp, 1hdc in next 3 sts. (8 sts)

Work edging:
Turn and make 32sc sts along the first side, 3sc into corner st, 22sc sts along bottom edge, 3sc into corner st, 32sc sts along second side. Fasten off.

flowers (make 4)

Use two colors for each flower.
Using first color and F/5 (4mm) hook, 6ch, join with a ss into first ch. Make 16sc into circle, joining tail around into each st, join with a ss. Fasten off.
Join second color into fastened off st.
*3ch, make 1dc into next two sts, 3ch, ss into next st; rep from * 4 more times. (5 petals)
Fasten off.
Pull tail to close up center hole and sew in ends.

lining

Block crocheted piece. Cut a piece of lining fabric the same size and shape, plus an extra ⅝in. (1.5cm) hem allowance all round. Pin, press, and machine or hand sew hems of lining. Match up buttonhole position on crocheted piece and make corresponding buttonhole on lining.

to make up

With RS of lining facing, pin onto WS of crocheted piece. Hand sew lining in place, ensuring that the buttonhole matches up. With RS of lining facing, turn bottom edge up to start of flap (decrease sides). Using a length of yarn, sew side seams of purse, leaving the flap open. Sew on button to correspond with buttonhole. Sew three flowers onto front and one onto back of purse.

Round Stripy Pillow Cover

Crochet is perfect for making circles and this pillow cover is a project I've been teaching to all my beginner students for many years, because it is beautiful and easy to make. It uses simple double stitch and the gorgeous range of Amy Butler colors from Rowan Yarns.

level 1: Beginner

materials

Rowan Belle Organic worsted/Aran (50% organic wool, 50% cotton)
1 x 50g ball (98yds/90m) each of:
209 Robin's Egg (A)
203 Orchid (B)
205 Rose (C)
212 Zinc (D)
206 Poppy (E)
211 Cilantro (F)
H/8 (5mm) crochet hook
16in. (40cm) round pillow form

abbreviations

ch chain
cont continue
dc double crochet
sc single crochet
ss slip stitch
WS wrong side

finished measurement

To fit a 16in. (40cm) diameter pillow form

gauge

14dc x 8 rows over a 4in. (10cm) square, using H/8 (5mm) hook.

method (make 2 sides)

Using A, make 6ch, join with ss into first ch.
Round 1: 3ch (counts as first dc), 11dc into circle, join with a ss into top of first 3-ch.
Change to B.
Round 2: 3ch, 1dc into same st, 2dc into every st to end of round, join with a ss into top of first 3-ch. (24 sts)
Change to C.
Round 3: 3ch, 1dc into same st, *1dc into next st, 2dc into next 2 sts; rep from * to last 2 sts, 1dc into next st, 2dc into last st, join with a ss into top of first 3-ch. (40 sts)
Change to D.
Round 4: 3ch, 1dc into same st, *1dc into next 3 sts, 2dc into next st; rep from *to last 3 sts, 1dc into each of last 3 sts, join with a ss into top of first 3-ch. (50 sts)
Change to E.
Round 5: 3ch, 1dc into same st, *1dc into next 4 sts, 2dc into next st; rep from * to last 4 sts, 1dc into each of last 4 sts, join with ss into top of first 3-ch. (60 sts)
Change to F.
Round 6: 3ch, 1dc into same st, *1dc into next 5 sts, 2dc into next st; rep from *to last 5 sts, 1dc into each of last 5 sts, join with a ss into top of first 3-ch. (70 sts)
Change to A.
Round 7: 3ch, 1dc into same st, *1dc into next 6 sts, 2dc into next st; rep from * to last 6 sts, 1dc into each of last 6 sts, join with a ss into top of first 3-ch. (80 sts)
Change to B.
Round 8: 3ch, 1dc into same st, *1dc into next 7 sts, 2dc into next st; rep from *to last 7 sts, 1dc into each of last 7 sts, join with a ss into top of first 3-ch. (90 sts)
Change to C.
Round 9: 3ch, 1dc into same st, *1dc into next 8 sts, 2dc into next st; rep from * to last 8 sts, 1dc into each of last 8 sts, join with a ss into top of first 3-ch. (100 sts)
Change to D.
Round 10: As Round 5. (120 sts)
Change to E.
Round 11: 3ch, 1dc into same st, *1dc into next 11 dc, 2dc in next st; rep from * to last 11 dc, 1dc into last 11 dc, join with a ss into top of first 3-ch. (130 sts)
Change to F.
Round 12: 3ch, 1dc into same st, *1dc into next 12 dc, 2dc in next st; rep

from * to last 12 dc, 1dc into last 12 dc, join with a ss into top of first 3-ch. Change to A.

Round 13: As Round 7.
Change to B.

Round 14: 3ch, 1dc into same st, *1dc into next 15 dc, 2dc in next st, rep from * to last 15 dc, 1dc into last 15 dc, join with a ss into top of first 3-ch. Change to C.

Round 15: 3ch, 1dc into same st, *1dc into next 16 dc, 2dc in next st; rep from * to last 16 dc, 1dc into last 16 dc, join with a ss into top of first 3-ch. Change to D.

Round 16: As Round 9.

to make up

Put pillow sides WS facing. Insert hook into both sides and using A, make 1ch. Make 1sc into each st, putting hook through both sides and joining sides together, leaving a big enough gap to push through pillow form. Cont in sc until seam is fully joined together. Fasten off. Sew in ends.

Beanie Hat

This hat has a really good shape, so it looks good either with or without the flower. It will also work for both men and women.

level 2: Improver

materials
Rooster Almerino worsted/Aran (50% baby alpaca, 50% merino wool)
2 x 50g balls (206yds/188m) each of:
309 Ocean (A)
307 Brighton Rock (B)
F/5 (4mm) crochet hook
Yarn sewing needle

abbreviations
ch chain
ch sp chain space
hdc half double
sc single crochet
ss slip stitch
st(s) stitch(es)

special abbreviations
cl (cluster) Yarn over hook, insert hook into ch or st, pull yarn through work, yarn over hook, insert hook into same ch, pull yarn through work, yarn over hook, insert hook into same ch, pull yarn through work, pull yarn through all 7 loops on hook, 1ch.
hdc2tog Yarn over hook, insert hook into next st, yarn over hook, draw a loop through, insert hook into next st, draw a loop through, yarn over hook and pull through all 4 loops.

finished measurement
To fit an average adult head

gauge
Gauge is not critical on this project.

method

Using A, make 86ch, ss into first ch to form a ring.

Round 1: 1ch, 1sc in each ch to end, ss into first ch.

Rounds 2–5: 1ch, 1sc in each st to end, ss into first ch.

Rounds 6–9: 2ch, 1hdc in each st to end, ss into first 2-ch.

Round 10: *1cl in next st, 1ch, skip 1 st; rep from * to end, ss into top of first cl.

Round 11: 2ch, * 1hdc in top of cl, 1hdc in next ch sp; rep from * to end, ss into first 2-ch.

Round 12: 2ch, 1hdc in each st to end, ss into first 2-ch.

Round 13: 2ch, *1hdc in next 4 sts, hdc2tog; rep from * to end, ss into first 2-ch.

Round 14: 2ch, 1hdc in each st to end, ss into first 2-ch.

Round 15: Skip 1 st, *1cl in next st, 1ch, skip 1 st; rep from * to end.

Round 16: 2ch, *1hdc in top of cl, 1hdc in ch sp; rep from * to end, ss into first 2-ch.

Round 17: 2ch, *1hdc in next 3 sts, hdc2tog; rep from * to end, ss into first 2-ch.

Round 18: 2ch, *1hdc in each st to end, ss into first 2-ch.

Round 19: Rep Round 18.

Round 20: 2ch, *1hdc in next 2 sts, hdc2tog; rep from * to end, ss into first 2-ch.

Round 21: 2ch, 1hdc in each st to end, ss into first 2-ch.

Round 22: 2ch, *1hdc in next st, hdc2tog; rep from * to end, ss into first 2-ch.

Round 23: Rep Round 21.

Round 24: 2ch, *hdc2tog; rep from * to end, ss into first 2-ch.

Round 25: 2ch, 1hdc in each st to end, ss into first 2-ch.

Fasten off leaving a long tail.

flower

Using B, make 54ch.

Row 1: 1dc into 5th ch from hook, * 1ch, skip 1ch, (1dc, 1ch, 1dc) in next ch; rep from * to end.

Row 2: 3ch, 5dc in first ch sp, *1sc in next ch sp, 6dc in next ch sp; rep from *, ending with 6dc in last ch sp. (25 *shells*)

Fasten off, leaving a long tail for sewing flower together.

to make up

To finish hat, thread tail onto a yarn sewing needle, thread through remaining stitches and pull tightly, sew in end.

To finish flower, thread needle with yarn tail, weave down side of shell to bottom. Roll first shell tightly to form center bud. Stitch at base of shell with two stitches to hold in place. Roll remaining strip around bud to form flower, securing as you roll by stitching through layers of chains at bottom of flower. Sew flower onto side of hat.

Patchwork Bag

This bag is made up of simple squares joined together to make a front, back, sides, and bottom. It's a good size and is made using the lovely color palette from Belle, the Amy Butler range of Rowan organic wool.

level 2: Improver

materials

Rowan Belle Organic light worsted/DK (50% organic wool, 50% cotton)
3 x 50g balls (393yds/360m) 005 Basil (MC)
1 x 50g ball (131yds/120m) each of:
002 Cornflower
008 Peony
012 Tomato
009 Hibiscus
014 Robin's Egg
016 Cilantro
013 Moonflower
F/5 (4mm) crochet hook
Yarn sewing needle
30 x 40in. (75 x 100cm) lining fabric
4 x 36in. (10 x 92cm) fusible interfacing
Sewing needle and thread

abbreviations

ch chain
ch sp chain space
cont continue
dc double crochet
RS right side
sc single crochet
ss slip stitch
st(s) stitch(es)
WS wrong side

finished measurement

Approx. 12 x 12in. (30 x 30cm)

gauge

Gauge is not critical on this project.

method

squares (make 27)

Use different color combinations and change color for each round, always using MC for Rounds 4 and 5.
Using first color, 4ch, join with a ss.
Round 1: 3ch (counts as 1dc), 2dc into ring, *1ch, 3dc into ring; rep from * twice more, 1ch, ss into top of first 3ch.
Fasten off.
Round 2: Join 2nd color into fastened-off st, make ss into each of next 2 dc and next 1ch sp, 3ch, 4dc into same sp to make a corner, *1dc into top center st of next 3-dc group, 5dc into next ch sp to make another corner; rep from * twice more, 1dc into top center st of next 3-dc group, ss to top of 3ch.
Fasten off.
Round 3: Join 3rd color into top of center st of any corner group, 3ch, 5dc into same place to make corner, *3dc into top st of next single dc, 6dc into top center st of next corner group; rep from * twice, 3dc into top st of next single dc, ss to top of 3ch.
Fasten off.
Round 4: Join MC between 3rd and 4th dc of any corner group, 3ch, 5dc into same place for corner, *3dc in next sp, 3dc in next sp, 6dc into center of next corner group; rep from * twice more, 3dc in next sp, 3dc in next sp, ss to top of 3-ch. Do not fasten off.
Round 5: Cont in MC, 1ch, 1sc in top of next 2 sts, 3sc in next st, *1sc in next 11 sts, 3sc; rep from * twice more, 1sc in next 9 sts, ss to top of first sc.
Fasten off.

to make up

Using an sc seam, make two panels (front and back) of 3 x 3 squares. Add three squares down each side of one set. Join to other set, leaving one seam open. Join three squares across at the bottom of one set to form the base of the bag. Join to other panel and base of sides.

top edging

Join yarn to any stitch across top edge. Make a sc edging around top: at each of 4 corners, *skip 1 st, ss into next st and continue to make 1sc in each st until next corner. Rep from * for each corner.
Fasten off.

handles (make two)

Using MC, make 110ch.
1hdc in 2nd ch from hook, 1hdc in each ch to end.
Fasten off.
Change to next color, 1hdc in each st to end.
Fasten off.
Change to next color, make 1hdc in each st to end.
Fasten off.
Change to MC, make 1hdc in each st to end.
Fasten off.

lining

Measure crocheted bag across width and length in several places. (It should be approx. 12 x 12in./30.5 x 30.5cm). Add ⅝in. (1.5cm) for each side seam and 2in. (5cm) for top and bottom and cut 2 pieces of lining to match (approx. 13 x 14in./33 x 35.5cm) for front and back. Measure down one side of crocheted side panel, along bottom edge, and up second side panel. Add an extra 2in. (5cm) for top and bottom seams and ⅝in. (1.5cm) to width for side seams, and cut one long strip of fabric to match (approx. 40 x 5½in./100 x 14cm) for sides and bottom lining. Cut a piece of lining fabric 6½ x 8in./16.5 x 20cm) for pocket.

Fold over top of pocket lining twice by ⅝in. (1.5cm) each time, pin and press. Fold side and bottom seams over once by ⅝in. (1.5cm), pin and press. Sew top seam. Position pocket in center of front lining on RS, with RS upward. Sew in place.

Measure fusible interfacing against sides and bottom fabric strip and cut to same size. Place fabric RS upward on top of interfacing and press to fuse together. With RS together, pin strip down one side of front piece. Sew seam, stopping ⅝in. (1.5cm) before bottom corner. Turn corner: make a

small cut ⅝in. (1.5cm) across and ⅝in. (1.5cm) up from first corner of long piece of fabric across seam allowance. Turn fabric strip round corner. Pin next seam (bottom) and sew. Cut long fabric strip at corner as before. Turn round corner, pin strip along last side edge, and sew to end. Repeat on other side of sides and bottom strip to join to back piece. Finish seams.

Turn top of lining over to WS by approx. 1in. (4cm), so lining fits inside top edge of bag without showing above crocheted piece. Place lining in bag and pin top edge of lining to top edge of crocheted piece.

Measure crocheted handles, add ⅝in. (1.5cm) to each side and both ends, and cut two strips of lining fabric to this length (each approx. 28 x 2½in./ 71 x 6.5cm). Pin and press lining to fit just on inside of handle pieces. Hand sew in place.

attach handles
Handles should be attached in center of first and last square of front and back of bag. Place a pin 1½in. (4cm) from outside edge of each side panel of bag as a marker. With handle lining facing inwards, attach ends of handles approx. 2in. (5cm) down into bag, aligning outside edge of handle with the pin marker. Hand sew handles in place, using MC yarn, so that they are sandwiched between lining and crocheted piece. Repeat on same side with other end of same handle. Repeat for second handle on other side of the bag.

Using sewing thread, hand stitch lining to crochet bag around top edge, incorporating handles. Work a few stitches in each corner along bottom and sides to secure lining in position to crochet.

tip
If the fabric you want to use for the lining is not 40in. (100cm), cut two shorter pieces and join them together to make one long strip.

Rose Shopper

This easy, quick project, using single crochet throughout, is perfect as a shopper. The lining makes it stronger, but if you are not so handy at sewing, it still works brilliantly without one. The flowers are Improver level, so if these are above your skill, replace with some simple flowers from the Purse—see page 30.

level 1: Beginner—shopper
level 2: Improver—flowers

materials
Debbie Bliss Como (90% wool, 10% cashmere)
6 x 50g balls (276yds/252m) 24 Silver (A)
1 x 50g ball (46yds/42m) 18 Lime (B)
Rowan Belle Organic light worsted/DK (50% organic wool, 50% cotton)
1 x 50g ball (131yds/120m) 004 Persimmon (C)
Rooster Almerino worsted/Aran (50% baby alpaca, 50% merino wool)
1 x 50g ball (103yds/94m) 306 Gooseberry (D)
M/13 (9mm), K10½ (7mm), and G/6 (4.5mm) crochet hooks
Yarn sewing needle
19.5in. (1m) length of lining fabric for bag
28 x 5in. (72 x 15cm) piece of lining fabric for handles
Sewing needle and thread
1 large snap fastener

abbreviations
ch chain
cont continue
dc double crochet
rep repeat
RS right side
sc single crochet
ss slip stitch
st(s) stitch(es)
WS wrong side

finished measurement
Shopper approx. 13½ x 11½in. (34 x 29cm), handles 25in. (64cm)

gauge
Gauge is not critical on this project.

method

main bag (make 2 pieces)
Using A and M/13 (9mm) hook, make 25ch.
Next row: 1ch, 1sc to end.
Rep this row until bag measures 12½in. (32cm).
Fasten off.

edging
Work around top edge of bag. With RS facing and using B and M/13 (9mm) hook, join yarn in a corner st, *3ch, ss into third ch from hook, skip 1 st, 1sc into next st; rep from * to end. Ss into joining st.
Fasten off.

handles (make two)
Using A and K10½ (7mm) hook, make 5ch, turn, 1sc into second ch from hook, 1sc to end. (4 sts).
Next row: 1ch, 1sc in each st to end. (4 sts)
Cont working this row until handle measures approx. 26in. (66cm).
Fasten off.

flowers (make 4)
Using C and G/6 (4.5mm) hook, make 4ch, ss into first ch to make a ring.
Round 1: *1sc, 1dc, 1sc into ring; rep from * 3 more times. (4 petals)
Round 2: *2ch, from WS ss into base of second sc of next petal (pick up 2 loops); rep from * 3 more times. Slip last st into first ss. (4 loops)
Round 3: *4dc into next 2 ch sp, ss into same ch sp; rep from * 3 more times.
Fasten off.
Round 4: Cont working with same col. Working into back of petals and picking up two loops, join yarn at base of highest point of previous round, *3ch, ss into middle of base of next petal; rep from * 3 more times, slip last st into joining st.
Round 5: *8dc into next 3 ch sp, ss into next 3 ch sp; rep from * 3 more times, slip last st into joining st.
Fasten off.
Change to D.

Round 6: Working into back of petals and picking up two loops, join yarn into middle of base of petal (next 8dc) of previous round, *3ch, ss into middle of base of next petal; rep from * 3 more times, slip last st into joining st.
Round 7: *10dc into 3ch sp, ss into same 3ch sp; rep from * 3 more times.
Fasten off.

to make up
With WS facing join front and back by sewing up side and bottom seams, leaving top open.

lining
Measure straps and cut out handle lining same size as crocheted handle allowing ⅝in. (1.5cm) extra for each hem at the sides, top, and bottom. With WS facing, press, pin, and machine stitch hem of lining along both sides. Press. Place lining on crocheted handle, with WS facing crochet. Pin and hand stitch lining and crocheted handle together. Rep for second handle.

Place a pin 1in. (2.5cm) from each outside seam of bag as a marker. With handle lining facing inwards, attach ends of handles approx. 2in. (5cm) down into bag, aligning outside edge of handle with the pin marker. Hand stitch handles to main piece. Rep on same side with other end of same handle. Rep for second handle on other side of bag.

Cut two pieces of lining fabric to same size as bag, adding a ⅝in. (1.5cm) seam allowance to sides and base and 1in. (2.5cm) to top. With RS together, pin and machine stitch side and bottom seams. Trim bottom corners and press seams open. Turn lining RS out. Turn top edge over to WS by 1in. (2.5cm) and press. Insert lining in bag and pin in place around top. Hand stitch lining to main piece around top edge, incorporating handles.

Sew each flower at each handle point at top of bag. Sew large snap fastener on inside center of lining.

Fabric Seat Covers

These make great seat covers; they are worked with a giant crochet hook and strips of fabric joined together and take no time at all.

level 1: Beginner

materials
Approx. 70yds (64m) x 1in. (2.5cm) of fabric strip wound into 2 x 500g balls
Approx. 4½yds (4m) x 1in. (2.5cm) wide ribbon
3in. (8cm) diameter large crochet hook

abbreviations
ch chain
sc single crochet
sc2tog Insert hook into next st, draw a loop through, insert hook into next st, draw a loop through, pull through all 3 sts.
st(s) stitch(es)

finished measurement
Length 15in. (38cm)
Width at back 13in. (33cm)
Width at front 17in. (43cm)

gauge
Gauge is not critical on this project.

method
Make 12ch.
Row 1: 1sc in second ch from hook, 1sc in each ch to end.
Rows 2–5: 1ch (counts as 1sc), 1sc in each st to end. (12 sts)
Row 6: 1ch, sc2tog, 1sc in next 8 sts, sc2tog. (10 sts)
Rows 7–11: 1ch, 1sc in each st to end. (10 sts)
Fasten off.
Weave in ends.

to make up
Cut four pieces of ribbon approx. 39in. (1m) each length. Attach one piece in each corner of shorter edges.

Jam Pot Covers

These fun and original jam pot covers are really quick and suitable for beginners. You can use any yarn—this pattern works with either light worsted or worsted weight, although in worsted the cover will come up slightly bigger.

level 1: Beginner

materials

Colorway 1 (light pink)
Rooster Almerino light worsted/DK (50% baby alpaca, 50% merino wool)
1 x 50g ball (124yds/112.5m) of each of:
203 Strawberry Cream (A)
201 Cornish (B)
Approx. 16in. (40cm) pale blue rikrak braiding

Colorway 2 (lavender)
Debbie Bliss Cashmerino worsted/Aran (55% merino wool, 33% microfibre, 12% cashmere)
1 x 50g ball (98yds/90m) 019 Lilac (A)
Rooster Almerino light worsted/DK (50% baby alpaca, 50% merino wool)
1 x 50g ball (124yds/112.5m) 207 Gooseberry (B)
Approx. 16in. (40cm) white rikrak braiding

Colorway 3 (green)
Rowan Handknit Cotton light worsted/DK (100% cotton)
1 x 50g ball (93yds/85m) 219 Gooseberry (A)
Rooster Almerino light worsted/DK (50% baby alpaca, 50% merino wool)
1 x 50g ball (124yds/112.5m) 211 Brighton Rock (B)
Approx. 16in. (40cm) yellow bobble braiding

Colorway 4 (bright pink)
Rooster Almerino light worsted/DK (50% baby alpaca, 50% merino wool)
1 x 50g ball (124yds/112.5m) each of:
211 Brighton Rock (A)
201 Cornish (B)
Approx. 16in. (40cm) lime green bobble braiding

F/5 (4mm) crochet hook

abbreviations

ch chain
hdc half double
RS right side
sc single crochet
sc2tog Insert hook into next st, draw a loop through, insert hook into next st, draw a loop through, pull through all 3 sts.
ss slip stitch
st(s) stitch(es)
dc double crochet

finished measurement

Standard 6in. (15cm) diameter
Large 7in. (18cm) diameter

gauge

Gauge is not critical on this project.

method

Both sizes
Using A and F/5 (4mm) hook, make 2ch, 6sc in second ch from hook, join with a ss.
Round 1: 3ch (counts as first dc), make 1dc into same st as 3ch, 2dc into next and each st to end, join with a ss into top of first 3-ch. (*12 sts*)
Round 2: 3ch, make 1dc into same st as 3ch, 2dc into next and each st to end, join with a ss into top of first 3-ch. (*24 sts*)
Round 3: 3ch, make 2dc into each of next 2 sts; * 1dc into next st, 2dc in each of next 2 sts; rep from * to end, join with a ss into top of first 3-ch. (*40 sts*)
Round 4: 3ch, make 1dc into each of next 2 sts, *2dc, 1dc in each of next 3 sts; rep from * to last st, 2dc, join with a ss into top of first 3-ch. (*50 sts*)
Round 5: 3ch, make 1dc in next st, *2dc, 1dc in each of next 2 sts; rep from * to last st, 1dc, join with a ss into top of first 3-ch. (*66 sts*)

For large size only
Round 6: 3ch, make 1dc in each st, join with a ss into top of first 3ch. (*66 sts*)
Fasten off A and join B.

Round 7: With RS facing, skip 1 st, *5dc in next st, skip 1 st, ss; rep from
* to last st, ss.
Fasten off.

to make up
Place cover on top of jar lid and secure with a rubber band. Finish off by
tying braiding around top, making a knot to secure in place.

Wash Cloths

The pretty stitch on these cloths is a favorite of mine, and they are made in 100% cotton. They make a lovely gift for someone with a new home.

level 2: Improver

materials
Rowan Handknit Cotton light worsted/DK (100% cotton)
2 x 50g balls (186yds/170m) each of:
333 Antique
336 Sunflower
F/5 (4mm) crochet hook

abbreviations
ch chain
dc double crochet
RS right side
sc single crochet
ss slip stitch
st(s) stitch(es)

special abbreviation
cl (cluster) Yarn over hook, insert hook into ch or st, pull yarn through work, yarn over hook, insert hook into same ch, pull yarn through work, yarn over hook, insert hook into same ch, pull yarn through work, pull yarn through all 7 loops on hook.

finished measurement
Approx. 10½in. (27cm) square

gauge
Gauge is not critical on this project.

method
Make 36ch.
Row 1: *Skip 2ch, 1cl, 2ch, 1cl into next ch, 1ch; rep from * along row, ending with 1dc into last ch.
Row 2: 1ch, *2sc into next 2ch sp, 1sc into next 1ch sp; rep from * to last sp, 1sc.
Row 3: 3ch, 1cl into second st, 2ch, 1cl into same st, 1ch, *skip 2 sts, 1cl, 2ch, 1cl into next st, 1ch; rep from * along row, ending with a 1dc into last ch.
Rep Rows 2 and 3 until work measures approx. 10½in. (27cm) or is square. Fasten off.

edging
Using contrasting color, with RS facing, start in right-hand corner, join yarn, 1ch, 2sc in same st as joining st, 31sc along top edge, 4sc into corner st, 31sc along one side edge, 4sc into corner st, 31sc along bottom edge, 4sc into corner st, 31sc along other side edge, ss into first ch.
Fasten off.

to make up
Block, press, and sew in ends.

Egg Cozies

Keep your boiled eggs warm with these cute little cozies.
Quick to make in the round and using organic yarn, they are
perfect gifts or breakfast table treats. Beginners will find
these easy and a good way to learn to crochet in the
round. Make them with a contrasting border; Improvers can
try some beading and bead around the bottom instead.

level 1: Beginner—without beads
level 2: Improver—with beads

materials
Rowan Belle Organic light worsted/DK (50% organic wool, 50% cotton)
1 x 50g ball (131yds/120m) each of:
012 Tomato
009 Hibiscus
014 Robin's Egg
016 Cilantro
Rooster Almerino light worsted/DK (50% baby alpaca, 50% merino wool)
1 x 50g ball (124yds/112.5m) 210 Custard
E/4 (3.5mm) crochet hook
Sewing needle and thread
2½in. (6cm) lengths x ½in. (1.5cm) wide ribbon for each cozy
15 x Rowan beads J3001016 (optional)

abbreviations
ch chain
rep repeat
sc single crochet
sc2tog Insert hook into next st, draw a loop through, insert hook into next st, draw a loop through, pull through all 3 sts.
ss slip stitch
st(s) stitch(es)

finished measurement
6in. (15.5cm) diameter

gauge
Gauge is not critical on this project.

method
without beads
Make 2ch, 6sc into second ch from hook.
Round 1: 2sc in each st to end. (12 sts)
Round 2: 2sc in each st to end. (24 sts)
Rounds 3–7: 1sc in each st.
Round 8: *1sc, sc2tog; rep from * to end. (16 sts)
If using a contrasting color, fasten off here and rejoin new color into fastened off st.
Round 9: 1sc in each st, ss into last st.
Fasten off.
Turn cozy right side out.

with beads
Thread 15 beads onto yarn before starting cozy.
Rep Rounds 1–8 of cozy pattern.

Beaded round
Work next round very loosely.
Round 9: Place bead to back of each st and make 1sc in each st, ss into last st.
Fasten off.
Turn cozy with beads on outside.

to make up
Sew in ends.
Cut a piece of ribbon 2½in. (6cm) long. Hem the two ends to prevent fraying and sew them together to make a tab. Sew onto top of each cozy.

Mug Warmers

This is a very simple little project and a fun way to liven up your breakfast table in the morning.

level 1: Beginner

materials

Colorway 1
Debbie Bliss Rialto worsted/Aran (100% merino wool)
1 x 50g ball (87.5yds/80m) 24 Pink

Colorway 2
Rooster Almerino worsted/Aran (50% baby alpaca, 50% merino wool)
1 x 50g ball (103yds/94m) 309 Ocean

G/6 (4.5mm) crochet hook
1 small button

abbreviations

ch chain
hdc half double
sc single crochet
ss slip stitch
st(s) stitch(es)

finished measurement

To fit a mug 3in. (7.5cm) diameter across the top

gauge

Gauge is not critical on this project.

method

Make 32ch.
Row 1: 1hdc in third ch from hook, 1hdc in each ch to end. (30 sts)
Row 2: 2ch, 1hdc in each st to end.
Row 3: 2ch, 2hdc in first st, 1hdc in each st to last st, 2hdc. (32 sts)
Row 4: 2ch, 2hdc in first st, 1hdc in each st to last st, 2hdc. (34 sts)
Row 5: 2ch, 1hdc in each st.
Row 6: 2ch, 1hdc in each st. At end of row, do not turn, make 8ch, ss approx. ½in. (1cm) down the side of work. Do not fasten off.

Edging:
Make 4sc evenly along first side edge, 3sc in corner st, 30sc along bottom edge, 3sc in corner st, 5sc along second side edge, 3sc in corner st, 1sc in each st across top, 1sc into each ch around button fastener, ss into first sc. Fasten off.

to make up

Sew side seam up to base of handle. Sew on button to correspond with button fastener. Place cup inside cover and fasten.

Cafetière Cozy

A fun and easy project to keep the coffee in your pot toastie and warm. The colors are changed at random as you work, for a multicolor effect.

level 1: Beginner

materials
Rooster Almerino worsted/Aran (50% baby alpaca, 50% merino wool)
1 x 50g ball (103yds/94m) each of:
305 Custard
310 Rooster
307 Brighton Rock
309 Ocean
302 Sugared Almond
303 Strawberry Cream
308 Spiced Plum
H/8 (5mm) crochet hook
Yarn sewing needle
1 small button

abbreviations
ch chain
rep repeat
RS right side
sc single crochet
ss slip stitch
st(s) stitch(es)
WS wrong side

finished measurement
To fit a medium-size 4–6 cup cafetière, approx. 12in. (31cm) circumference

gauge
16sc x 20 rows over 4in. (10cm) square, using H/8 (5mm) hook.

method
Using any color, make 46ch.
Row 1: 1sc into next ch from hook, 1sc into each ch to end, turn. (45 sts)
Row 2: 1ch, 1sc into each st to end.
Rep Row 2, changing colors randomly every 2, 3, or 4 rows, until work measures 6¼in. (16cm), or to just above handle of cafetière. Do not fasten off.

Make buttonhole and button tab:
Make 5ch, 1sc into next ch from hook, 1sc into each st to end, turn.
Next row: 1sc into each st to last 4 sts, make 2ch, skip 2 sts, 1sc into each of next 2 sts.
Next row: 1ch, 1sc into each of next 2 sts, 2sc into next ch sp, 1sc into each st to end.
Next row: 1sc into each st to end. Do not fasten off.
Work sc around button tab by making 2sc around side, 1sc in each of the sts underneath to end. Make ss into straight edge.
Fasten off.

to make up
With WS facing, sew a seam 1in. (2.5cm) up from the bottom, leaving the remainder open. Turn RS out. Sew a button to correspond with buttonhole. Sew in ends.

Peaked Toddler Hat

The little peak on this hat makes it a very cute version of the traditional beanie. The design is great for a girl or a boy.

level 1: Beginner

materials
Debbie Bliss Cashmerino worsted/Aran (55% merino wool, 33% microfibre, 12% cashmere)
1 x 50g ball (98yds/90m) 024 Green (A)
Debbie Bliss Rialto worsted/Aran (100% extra fine merino wool)
1 x 50g ball (87.5yds/80m) 034 Orange (B)
E/4 (3.5mm) crochet hook
Yarn sewing needle

abbreviations
beg beginning
ch chain
dc double
hdc half double
rep repeat
RS right side
sc single crochet
sc2tog Insert hook into next st, draw a loop through, insert hook into next st, draw a loop through, pull through all 3 sts.
ss slip stitch
st(s) stitch(es)

special abbreviation
hdc2tog Yarn over hook, insert hook into next st, yarn over hook, draw a loop through, insert hook into next st, draw a loop through, yarn over hook and pull through all 4 loops.

finished measurement
To fit a child approx. 18–36 months old

gauge
Gauge is not critical on this project.

method

Using A, make 80ch, join with ss into first ch to make a ring.

Round 1: 2ch, 1hdc in each ch, ss into first 2-ch.

Rounds 2-4: 2ch, 1hdc in each st, ss into first 2-ch.

Round 5: 1ch, 1sc in each st, join with ss into first ch.

Round 6: 1ch, *1sc in next 18 sts, sc2tog; rep from * to end, join with ss into first ch.

Round 7: Rep Round 5.

Round 8: 2ch, 1hdc in each st, ss into first 2-ch.

Round 9: 2ch, *1hdc in next 17 sts, hdc2tog; rep from * to end, ss into first 2-ch.

Rounds 10-11: Rep Round 8. (68 sts)

Round 12: 1ch, 1sc in next 6 sts, *sc2tog, 1sc in next 6 sts; rep from * to end, ss into first ch. (60 sts)

Rounds 13-14: Rep Round 5.

Round 15: 2ch, 1hdc in next 4 sts, hdc2tog; rep from * to end, ss into first 2-ch.

Round 16: Rep Round 8.

Round 17: 2ch, 1hdc in next 3 sts, hdc2tog; rep from * to end, ss into first 2-ch.

Round 18: 2ch, *1hdc in next 2 sts, hdc2tog; rep from * to last 3 sts, 1hdc, hdc2tog, ss into first 2-ch.

Round 19: 2ch, *1hdc in next st, hdc2tog; rep from * to end, ss into first 2-ch.

Round 20: 2ch, *1hdc in each st, ss into first 2-ch.

Round 21: 2ch, *hdc2tog; rep from * to end, ss into first 2-ch.

Fasten off.

peak

With RS of hat facing, count 21 sts from beg of first round to left. Join yarn in 22nd st, work 1sc into each of next 38 sts, turn.

Rows 1-3: Skip 1 st, 1sc in each st to last 2 sts, skip 1 st, 1sc in last st.

Row 4: Sc2tog twice, 1sc in each st to last 4 sts, sc2tog twice.

Row 5: Skip 1 st, 1sc in each st to last 2 sts, skip 1 st, 1sc in last st.

Row 6: Skip 1 st, sc2tog, 1sc in each st to last 4 sts, sc2tog, skip 1 st, 1sc in last st.

Row 7: Skip 1 st, 1sc in each st to last 2 sts, skip 1 st, 1sc in last st.

Row 8: Rep Row 7 until 14 sts remain.

Fasten off, leaving long strand of yarn for sewing peak.

flower

Using B, make 35ch.

Row 1: 1dc into fifth ch from hook, * 1ch, skip 1ch, (1dc, 1ch, 1dc) in next ch; rep from * to end.

Row 2: 3ch, 5dc in first ch sp, *1sc in next ch sp, 6dc in next ch sp; rep from *, ending with 6dc in last ch sp. (16 shells)

Fasten off, leaving a long tail for sewing flower together.

to make up

To finish peak, thread strand of yarn into yarn sewing needle, turn last two single crochet rows inwards, and sew to inside of peak to make a firm edge.

To finish flower, thread needle with yarn tail, weave down side of shell to bottom. Roll first shell tightly to form center bud. Stitch at base of shell with two stitches to hold in place and roll remaining strip around bud to form flower, securing as you roll by stitching through layers of chains at bottom of flower. Sew flower onto side of hat.

chapter 2

Practice makes perfect

Stripy Wave Pillow

This pillow is a great way to play with colors; I have used bright and cheerful tones in a very soft mix of alpaca and merino wool, but the design would also work well in seaside blues or soft pastels.

level 2: Improver

materials

Rooster Almerino worsted/Aran (50% baby alpaca, 50% merino wool)
1 x 50g ball (103yds/94m) each of:
305 Custard (A)
302 Sugared Almond (B)
307 Brighton Rock (C)
301 Cornish (D)
309 Ocean (E)
303 Strawberry Cream (F)
2 x 50g balls (206yds/188m) 306 Gooseberry (G)
G/6 (4.5mm) crochet hook
Yarn sewing needle
16in. (40cm) square pillow form

abbreviations

ch chain
dc double crochet
hdc half double
sc single crochet
ss slip stitch
st(s) stitches
WS wrong side

special abbreviation

dc3tog Yarn round hook, insert hook into next st, yarn round hook, draw a loop through, yarn round hook and draw through 2 loops on hook (2 loops left on hook). Rep this step into next st (3 loops on hook). Rep this step once more (4 loops on hook), draw yarn through all 4 loops.

finished measurement

To fit a 16in. (40cm) square pillow form

gauge

15dc x 8 rows over 4in. (10cm) square, using G/6 (4.5mm) hook.

method (make 2 sides)

Using A, make 63ch.

Row 1: 1dc into 2nd ch from hook, 1dc into next ch, *1dc into each of next 3 ch, dc3tog over next 3 ch, 1dc in next 3-ch, 3dc in next st; rep from * ending last rep with 2dc into last ch, turn.

Row 2: 3ch, 1dc into first st, *1dc into each of next 3 sts, dc3tog over next 3 sts, 1dc into each of next 3 sts, 3dc in next st; rep from *, ending last rep with 2dc into top of turning chain, turn.

Change to next color.

*Rep Row 2 twice and change color; rep from *, changing color every two rows.

Continue until work measures 15in. (37.5cm). Fasten off.

edging

Round 1: With RS facing, join F into fastened-off st.

Side 1:

1ch, 1sc into each of next 2 sts, 1hdc in each of next 2 sts, 1dc into next 3 sts, 1hdc into next 2 sts, *1sc into next 3 sts, 1hdc into next 2 sts, 1dc into next 3 sts, 1hdc into next 2 sts; rep from * to last 2 sts, 1sc in next st, 4sc in corner st.

Side 2:

*Make 4sc into each color for 6 rows, 5sc evenly in next two rows; rep from * to last two colors, 4sc in each color. (63 sts)

Side 3:

Working on bottom ch from Row 1 of pillow cover, 1dc in next 2 sts, 1hdc in next 2 sts; rep from * from side 1 to last 6 sts. 1sc in next 3 sts, 2hdc, 1dc, 4sc in corner st.

Side 4:

Repeat side 2, making last 2 sts into corner st. Join with a ss into first ch from side 1. (63 sts)

Round 2: 1sc into each st around pillow cover, 4sc in each corner st. Join with a ss into first st. (252 sts)

Round 3: Rep Round 2.

Fasten off.

to make up

Sew in ends.

Round 1: Place pillow covers WS together, join G into any st. Make 1sc into each st, 4sc in each corner st, along three sides. Insert pillow form, continue to make 1sc in each st to end.

Round 2: 1sc into each st around pillow cover, 4sc in each corner st, join with a ss into first st.

Fasten off.

Sew in ends.

tips

Using one of the strong colors for the sc seam will define the outline of the pillow and ties the other colors together.

The increases and decreases should be in line with each other from the previous row—check the alignment as you work. This will ensure that you achieve the 'wave' effect in the pattern.

Baby Blanket

A really beautiful blanket, made with a pretty soft fan stitch
and frilled edging—an ideal gift for a newborn.

level 2: Improver

materials

Rooster Baby Rooster (100% fine merino)
8 x 50g balls (1096yds/1000m) 407 Vintage Rose (A)
1 x 50g ball (137yds/125m) 400 Cornish (B)
2 x 50g balls (274yds/250m) 402 Parma Violet (C)
E/4 (3.5mm) crochet hook

abbreviations

ch chain
dc double crochet
hdc half double
rep repeat
RS right side
sc single crochet
ss slip stitch
st(s) stitch(es)

special abbreviation

dc3tog Yarn round hook, insert hook into next st,
yarn round hook, draw a loop through, yarn
round hook and draw through 2 loops on hook
(2 loops left on hook). Rep this step into next st
(3 loops on hook). Rep first step once more
(4 loops on hook), draw yarn through 4 loops.

finished measurement

Approx. 26 x 35in. (66 x 89cm)

gauge

Gauge is not critical on this project.

method

Using E/4 (3.5mm) hook and A, make 123 ch.
Row 1: 1dc into second ch from hook, 1dc into next ch, *1dc into each of
next 3 ch, dc3tog over next 3 ch, 1dc into each of next 3 ch, 3dc into next
ch; rep from *, ending row with 2dc into last ch.
Row 2: 3ch, 1dc into first st, *1dc into each of next 3 sts, dc3tog over next
3 sts, 1dc into each of next 3 sts, 3dc into next st; rep from * until last 3 sts,
1dc in each st, 2dc into top of turning chain.
Rep Row 2 until work measures approx. 34in. (87cm).
Fasten off.

edging

Round 1: With RS facing, join col B into fastened-off st.

Side 1:
1ch, 1sc into each of next 2 sts, 1hdc, 1dc into next 2 sts, 1hdc into next
3 sts, *1sc into next 3 sts, 1hdc into next 2 sts, 1dc into next 3 sts, 1hdc into
next 2 sts; rep from * to last 2 sts, 1sc in next st, 3sc in corner st. (*125 sts*)

Side 2:
Make 152sc along side to end, make 3sc in corner st. (*155 sts*)

Side 3:
Working on bottom of ch from Row 1 of blanket, 1dc in next 2 sts, 1hdc in
next 2 sts; rep from * to * from side 1, 1hdc, 1dc, 1hdc, 1sc in last st.
(*125 sts*)

Side 4:
Repeat side 2, making last 2 sts into corner st, join with a ss into first ch from
side 1. (*155 sts*)

Round 2: 3ch, 1hdc into each st around blanket, 4hdc in first 3 corner sts,
5hdc into last corner st, join with ss into first st. (*576 sts*)
Fasten off.
Change to C.
Round 3: With RS facing, join yarn into fastened-off st from previous round,
*1ch, skip 1 st, [1sc, 1ch, 1hdc] in next st, skip 1 st, [1dc, 1ch, 1dc] in next
st, skip 1 st, [1hdc, 1ch, 1sc] in next st, 1ch, skip 1 st, ss in next st; rep from
* to end, ss last stitch into first ch. Do not fasten off.
Round 4: *1sc, 1hdc in next ch sp, 3dc in next sp (between sc and hdc
from previous round), [3tr, 1ch, 3tr] in next ch sp (between doubles from
previous round), 3dc in next sp (between hdc and sc from previous round),
[1hdc, 1sc] in next ch sp, ss in same st as ss from previous row; rep from
* to end.
Fasten off.

Chunky Seashell Scarf

Chunky scarves are really popular in all the high street fashion shops, so why not make your own? This project uses beautifully soft chunky wool, has a really contemporary designer look and only takes a couple of evenings to make—what could be better!

level 2: Improver

materials

Debbie Bliss Como (90% wool, 10% cashmere)
7 x 50g balls (322yds/294m) 06 Duck Egg
K10½ (7mm) crochet hook

abbreviations

ch chain
ch sp chain space
sc single crochet
ss slip stitch
st(s) stitch(es)
tr treble crochet

finished measurement

Approx. 10in. (25.5cm) wide x 58in. (148cm) long

gauge

Gauge is not critical on this project.

method

Make 20ch very loosely.

Row 1: Working very loosely on this row, 1sc into second ch from hook and in each of following ch to end.

Row 2: 1sc into first st, *skip 4 sts, 7tr in next st, 1sc in next st; rep from * to end.

Row 3: 4ch, 1tr into first sc from previous row, *3ch, skip 3 sts, 1sc in top of next st (top of fan), 3ch, skip 3 sts, 2tr into top of sc from last row (between shells); rep from *, ending row with 2tr in last sc of previous row.

Row 4: 1ch, 1sc in next st, *skip next ch sp, make 7tr into top of sc from previous row, skip 3ch, 1sc in sp between 2tr from previous row; rep from *, ending row with 1sc in sp between last tr and turning ch.

Rep Rows 3 and 4 until scarf measures approx. 57½in. (146.5cm), ending with a Row 4.

Last row: 1ch, *1sc into each 7tr from previous row, 1ch, 1sc between shells, 1ch; rep from * to end, finishing with 1ch, ss into last st.

Fasten off. Sew in ends.

Floral Curtain Tie-Backs

These curtain ties use very little yarn, so you can use up scraps of any type left over from another project.

level 1: Beginner

materials

Debbie Bliss Cashmerino light worsted/DK (55% merino wool, 33% microfibre, 12% cashmere)
1 x 50g ball (120yds/110m) 011 Green (A)
Rooster Almerino light worsted/DK (50% baby alpaca, 50% merino wool)
1 x 50g ball (124yds/112.5m) each of:
211 Brighton Rock (B)
201 Cornish (C)
F/5 (4mm) crochet hook
Yarn sewing needle

abbreviations

ch chain
dc double crochet
dtr double treble
rep repeat
sc single crochet
ss slip stitch
st(s) stitch(es)
tr treble crochet

finished measurement

Makes two tie-backs each approx. 43in. (110cm)

gauge

Gauge is not critical on this project.

method

Each tie-back has 2 x small roses, 1 x large rose, and 5 petal flowers.

petal flower (make 10)

Using A, make 6ch, join with ss into first ch.
Make 16sc into circle, joining tail into each sc round circle, join with a ss.
Change to B.

*3ch, 1dc into next 2 sts, 3ch, ss into next st; rep from * 4 more times.
(5 petals)
Fasten off.
Pull tail to close up center hole and sew in ends.

small roses (make 4)

Make 48ch.
Petals 1–3: Skip 3ch, 1dc in each of next 2ch, 2ch, ss in next ch *3ch, 1dc in each of next 2 ch, 2ch, ss in next ch; rep from * to end once more.
(3 petals)
Petals 4–6: *4ch, 1tr in each of next 4 ch, 3ch, ss in next ch; rep from * twice more.
Petals 7–9: *4ch, 1tr in each of next 6 ch, 3ch, ss in next ch; rep from * twice more.
Fasten off.

Large roses (make 2)

Make 99ch.
Petals 1–4: Skip 3ch, 1dc in each of next 2 ch, 2ch, ss in next ch, [3ch, 1dc in each of next 2 ch, 2ch, ss in next ch] 3 times.
Petals 5–8: [4ch, 1tr in each of next 4 ch, 3ch, ss in next ch] 4 times.
Petals 9–12: [4ch, 1tr in each of next 6 ch, 3ch ss in next ch] 4 times.
Petals 13–16: [5ch, 1dtr in each of next 8ch, 4ch, ss in next ch] 4 times.
Fasten off.

to make up

To make roses, press petals flat. Starting with smaller petals, coil petals, keeping base flat at chain edge and stitch in place as you go.

Make two lengths of chains for each tie-back, each 21in. (54cm) long. Fasten off. Attach one end of one chain to back of one small rose, leave 4in. (10cm) gap, then attach chain to back of large rose. Make 1in. (2.5cm) loop at other end of chain and secure in place. Attach one end of other chain to back of other small rose, leave 3in. (7.5cm) gap, and attach chain to back of large rose. Cross second chain over top of first chain and attach in place, so chains are secured and crossed at back. Place five petal flowers evenly along chain and attach, leaving 1in. (2.5cm) gap between each one and allowing enough space at other end for 1in. (2.5cm) loop as first chain. Rep for second tie-back.

Felted Beaded Bracelet

This very pretty bracelet must be made using 100% pure wool, so that it will felt correctly. It's felted by washing it in the washing machine before sewing on the beads.

level 2: Improver

materials

Cascade 220 light worsted/DK (100% Peruvian wool)
1 x 100g hank (220yds/200m) 7802 Bright Pink
F/5 (4mm) crochet hook
1in. (2cm) wide ribbon x wrist measurement plus ½in. (1.5cm) at each end for hem
1in. (2cm) wide pink felt x wrist measurement
Sewing needle and thread
9 seed beads
1 small snap fastener

abbreviations

ch chain
dc double crochet
sc single crochet
ss slip stitch
st(s) stitch(es)
WS wrong side

finished measurement

1in. (2cm) wide x wrist circumference

gauge

Gauge is not critical on this project.

method

flowers (make 3)

Make 5ch, join with a ss to make a ring.
Round 1: *1sc, 1dc, 1sc into ring; rep from * 3 more times. (4 petals)
Round 2: *2ch, from WS ss into base of second sc of next petal (pick up 2 loops); rep from * 3 more times, slip last st into joining st. (4 loops)
Round 3: *4dc into next 2 ch sp at back, ss into same ch sp; rep from * 3 more times.
Fasten off.

to make up

Place flowers in the washing machine on a 60ºC wash. Allow to dry naturally.

Sew three beads into center of each flower. Sew flowers in a group on center of ribbon. Hem each end of ribbon. Sew felt to back of ribbon. Sew snap fastener in place.

Fingerless Gloves

These delicate fingerless gloves are charming and are also a good project to try out some edging skills.

level 2: Improver

materials

Debbie Bliss Cashmerino light worsted/DK (55% merino wool, 33% microfibre, 12% cashmere)
2 x 50g balls (240yds/220m) 022 Raspberry Pink
E/4 (3.75mm) crochet hook

abbreviations

ch chain
dc double crochet
inc including
rep repeat
sc single crochet
ss slip stitch
st(s) stitch(es)

finished measurement

To fit an average size woman's hand

gauge

Gauge is not critical on this project.

method

glove (make 2)

Make 36ch, join with ss into first ch to make a ring.
Round 1: 1ch, skip 1 ch, 1sc in each of next 35ch, join with a ss into next ch. (35 sts)
Round 2: 6ch, skip 3 sts, 1dc, *3ch, skip 3 sts, 1dc; rep from * six times, 3ch, ss into third of first 6ch. (9 spaces)
Round 3: 1ch, skip 1 st, 1sc in each of next 35 sts, join with a ss into next st. (35 sts)
Rounds 4–9: Rep Round 3. (35 sts)
Round 10: 1ch, *skip 1 st, 1sc in each of next 4 sts; rep from * to last 2 sts, 1sc in next st, join with a ss into next st. (29 sts)

Round 11: 1ch, skip 1 st, *1sc in each of next 29 sts, join with a ss into next st. (29 sts)
Round 12: 1ch, skip 1 st, *1sc in each of next 3 sts, 2sc in next st; rep from * to last st, join with a ss into next st. (36 sts)
Rounds 13–21: Rep Round 3. (36 sts)
Round 22 (left glove only): 1ch, skip 1 st, 1sc in each of next 2 sts, 5ch, skip 5 sts, 1sc in next st, 1sc in each st to last st, join with a ss into next st.
Round 22 (right glove only): 1ch, skip 1 st, 1sc in each st to last 7 sts, 5ch, skip 5 sts, 1sc in next 2 sts, join with a ss into next st.
Round 23: 1ch, skip 1 st, 1sc in each st (including into each 5ch from previous round), join with a ss into next st. (36 sts)
Rounds 24–26: 1ch, skip 1 st, 1sc into next 36 sts, join with a ss into next st. (36 sts)
Round 27: 1ch, *skip next st, 1sc in each of next 8 sts; rep from * twice more, skip next st, 1sc in each st to last st, join with a ss into next st. (33 sts)
Rounds 28–30: Rep Round 3. (33 sts)
Round 31: *5ch, skip 3 sts, 1sc into next st; rep from * 7 times more, 3ch, 1dc into base of first 5-ch.
Round 32: *5ch, 1sc into 3rd of 5-ch from previous round; rep from * 7 times more, 3ch, 1dc into top of dc from previous round.
Round 33: Rep Round 32 to last sc, 5ch, ss into top of first 5-ch from previous round.
Fasten off.

thumb

Rejoin yarn to thumbhole created by Rounds 22–23.
Round 1: 1ch, 1sc into each of 5 sts at top of hole, make 1sc in each of 5 sts at bottom of thumbhole, join with a ss into first ch.
Round 2: 1ch, skip 1 st, 1sc in next 9 sts, join with a ss into next st.
Rounds 3–5: Rep Round 2.
Fasten off.

edging

Join yarn into start st at wrist end of glove.
Round 1: *5ch, skip 5 sts, 1sc into next st; rep from * to end.
Round 2: *5dc into first ch sp, ss into next sc from previous round; rep from * to end. Ss into base of first 5dc.
Fasten off.
Sew in ends.

> **tip**
> To achieve a straight seam with this project, take care when counting stitches in each round.

Swishy Scarf

This scarf is made with half doubles in the middle and is crocheted horizontally, with a lacy edging. If you are a beginner, make 4–5 rows more of half doubles than in the pattern, if you are an intermediate, have a go at the pretty edging.

level 2: Improver

materials
Rooster Almerino light worsted/DK (50% baby alpaca, 50% merino wool)
3 x 50g balls (372yds/337.5m) 201 Cornish
F/5 (4mm) crochet hook

abbreviations
ch chain
ch sp chain space
dc double crochet
hdc half double
sc single crochet
ss slip stitch
st(s) stitch(es)
tr treble crochet

finished measurement
Approx. 62 x 4½in. (157 x 11cm)

gauge
Gauge is not critical on this project.

method
Make 258ch.
Row 1: 1hdc in second ch from hook, 1hdc in each ch to end.
Rows 2–3: 2ch, 1hdc in each st to end. Do not fasten off.

Edging:
Work in rounds, not in rows. Do not turn at end of round.
Round 1: *3ch, skip 3 sts, 1sc into next st**; rep from * to ** until first corner, 3ch, 1sc into middle of second row of side edge, 3ch, 1sc into next corner; rep from * to ** to next corner, 3ch, 1sc into middle of second row of side edge, 3ch, join with ss into base of first 3-ch.
Round 2: 2dc, 3ch, 2dc into middle st of first 3-ch from previous round. *2dc, 3ch, 2dc into middle st of next 3-ch from previous round; rep from * to end of round, join with ss into top of first 2-dc.
Round 3: Ss into middle st of first 3-ch from previous round, *5ch, ss into middle st of next 3-ch from previous round; rep from * to end, 5ch, ss into first ss.
Round 4: *5sc into 5ch sp; rep from * to end, join with ss into ss from previous round.
Round 5: *1sc into first st, 1ch, 1hdc, 1ch, 1dc into next st, [1ch, 1tr, 1ch] 3 times into next st, 1dc, 1ch, 1hdc into next st, 1ch, 1sc into next st, ss into ss from previous round; rep from * to end, join with ss into ss from previous round. Fasten off.
Sew in ends.

Baby Bouncers

Little crochet balls for tiny hands; lovely for babies to hold, throw or crawl after. These are great to practice crocheting in the round. Make them using one color or with stripes.

level 1: Beginner

materials
Small amounts of each of:
King Cole Merino Blend light worsted/DK (100% merino wool)
55 Gold
787 Fuchsia

Debbie Bliss Cashmerino light worsted/DK (55% merino wool, 33% microfibre, 12% cashmere)
017 Lilac
029 Light Green
Rowan Belle Organic light worsted/DK
(50% organic wool, 50% cotton)
014 Robin's Egg
Rooster Almerino light worsted/DK
(50% baby alpaca, 50% merino wool)
203 Strawberry Cream

4mm (F/5) crochet hook
Fiberfill stuffing

abbreviations
beg beginning
ch chain
sc single crochet
sc2tog Insert hook into next st, draw a loop through, insert hook into next st, draw a loop through, pull through all 3 sts.
ss slip stitch
st(s) stitch(es)

finished measurement
3in. (7.5cm) diameter

gauge
Gauge is not critical on this project.

method
Place st marker at beg of each round.
Round 1: 2ch, 6sc into second ch from hook.
Round 2: 2sc in each st. (*12 sts*)
Round 3: *1sc in next st, 2sc; rep from * to end. (*18 sts*)
Round 4: *1sc in next 2 sts, 2sc; rep from * to end. (*24 sts*)
Round 5: *1sc in next 3 sts, 2sc; rep from * to end. (*30 sts*)
Rounds 6-10: 1sc in each st. (*30 sts*)
Round 11: *1sc in next 3 sts, sc2tog; rep from * to end. (*24 sts*)
Round 12: *1sc in next 2 sts, sc2tog; rep from * to end. (*18 sts*)
Round 13: *1sc in next st, sc2tog; rep from * to end. (*12 sts*)
Stuff ball.
Round 14: Sc2tog around until hole closes.
Fasten off.
Sew in ends.

Chunky Luscious Pillow

This gorgeous pillow is made using a hand-dyed chunky wool in beautiful soft tones. It uses a fairly large hook and thick yarn, so takes no time at all to make.

level 2: Improver

materials

Fyberspates Scrumptious Chunky (45% silk, 55% wool)
5 x 100g hanks (667yds/610m) Copper Spring
J/10 (6mm) crochet hook
Yarn sewing needle
3 x 1½in. (4cm) buttons
18in. (45.5cm) square pillow form

abbreviations

ch chain
dc double crochet
rep repeat
sc single crochet
ss slip stitch
st(s) stitch(es)

special abbreviation

dc3tog Yarn round hook, insert hook into next st, yarn round hook, draw a loop through, yarn round hook and draw through 2 loops on hook (2 loops left on hook). Rep this step into next st (3 loops on hook). Rep first step once more (4 loops on hook), draw yarn through all 4 loops.

finished measurement

To fit a 18in. (45.5cm) square pillow form

gauge

13dc x 7 rows over 4in. (10cm) square, using J/10 (6mm) hook.

method

Make 51ch.

Row 1: 1dc in fourth ch from hook, 1dc in next ch (dc2tog over next 2ch) twice, 1dc in next ch, 2dc in next ch, *2dc in next ch, 1dc in next ch, (dc2tog over next 2ch) twice, 1dc in next ch, 2dc in next ch; rep from * to end.

Row 2: 3ch, 1dc in first dc, 1dc in next dc, (dc2tog over next 2 sts) twice, 1dc in next dc, 2dc in next dc, *2dc in next dc, 1dc in next dc, (dc2tog over next 2 sts) twice, 1dc in next dc, 2dc in next dc; rep from * to first 3ch, work last 2dc into third of first 3ch.

Rep Row 2 until work measures 39in. (99cm).

Next row: 3ch, 1dc in first dc, 1dc in next dc, (dc2tog over next 2 sts) twice, 1dc in next dc, *4ch, skip 2 sts, 1dc in next dc, (dc2tog over next 2 sts) twice, 1dc in next dc, 2dc in each of next 2dc, 1dc in next dc, (dc2tog over next 2 sts) twice, 1dc in next dc*; rep from * to*, 4ch, skip next 2 sts, 1dc in next dc, (dc2tog over next 2 sts) twice, 1dc in next dc, 2dc in next dc, turn.

Work 2 more rows as Row 2, working into each of 4-ch as if a dc.

to make up

With RS facing, fold from bottom to 4in. (10cm) from top. Fold top flap so it overlaps bottom. Ensure pillow cover measures 18in. (45.5cm). Sc side seams together. Sew on buttons to correspond with buttonholes.

Baby Bibs

These cute, pretty bibs are made using a 100% cotton yarn, so it's easy to wash off mucky mealtime mayhem.

level 2: Improver

materials

Colorway 1
Rowan Handknit Cotton light worsted/DK (100% cotton)
1 x 50g ball (93yds/85m) each of:
303 Sugar (A)
251 Ecru (B)
Debbie Bliss Cotton light worsted/DK (100% cotton)
1 x 50g ball (92yds/84m) 49 Mauve (C)

Colorway 2
Debbie Bliss Cotton light worsted/DK (100% cotton)
1 x 50g ball (92yds/84m) each of:
51 Sky (A)

09 Duck Egg Blue (C)
Rowan Handknit Cotton light worsted/DK (100% cotton)
1 x 50g ball (93yds/85m) 251 Ecru (B)

D/3 (3mm) and F/5 (4mm) crochet hooks

abbreviations
ch chain
sc single crochet
sc2tog Insert hook into next st, draw a loop through, insert hook into next st, draw a loop through, pull through all 3 sts.
ss slip stitch
st(s) stitch(es)

finished measurement
Approx. 13 x 19cm (5¼ x 7½in)

gauge
Gauge is not critical on this project.

method

Using F/5 (4mm) hook and A, make 21ch.

Row 1: 1sc into next ch from hook, 1sc in each ch to end. (20 sts)

Row 2: 1ch, 1sc in each st to end. (20 sts)

Rows 3–5: 1ch, 2sc in first st, 1sc in each st to last st, 2sc. (26 sts)

Change to B.

Row 6: 1sc in each st to end. (26 sts)

Row 7: 1ch, 1sc in each st to end.

Change to A.

Row 8: 1sc in each st to end.

Change to B.

Rows 9–10: 1sc in each st to end.

Change to A.

Rows 11–15: 1sc in each st to end.

Change to B.

Rows 16–17: 1sc in each st to end.

Change to A.

Row 18: 1sc in each st to end.

Rows 19–20: 1ch, 1sc in each st to end.

Neck edge

Row 21: 1ch, 1sc in each of next 7 sts, turn. (7 sts)

Row 22: 1ch, sc2tog, 1sc in each of next 3 sts, sc2tog. (5 sts)

Row 23: 1ch, sc2tog, 1sc in next st, sc2tog. (3 sts)

Rows 24–25: 1ch, 1sc in each st. (3 sts)

Row 26: 1ch, skip 1 st, 1sc.

Row 27: 1ch, sc2tog.

Fasten off.

Join A to other edge of bib.

Row 1: 1ch, 1sc in each of next 7 sts. (7 sts)

Rows 2–7: Same as Rows 22–27

Fasten off.

Edging

Bottom edge

Turn bib upside down and start edging by working from bottom. Using F/5 (4mm) hook and C, join yarn in bottom right-hand corner, make 18sc.

Side edge 1

Skip one sp, make ss into next space, 26sc up side edging to tip. Do not fasten off.

Tie 1

35ch, 1sc in second ch from hook, 1sc in next 33 ch.

Neck edge

8sc along first curve, 13sc along straight edge, 8sc along second curve. Do not fasten off.

Tie 2

35ch, 1sc in second ch from hook, 1sc in next 33 ch.

Side edge

26sc down side edging. Skip last space and make ss into first sc from bottom edge. Do not fasten off.

Using D/3 (3mm) hook, make 1sc into each st around side, ties, and neck edgings, join with a ss into first sc.

Baby Slippers

I originally saw a pattern for similar slippers in a vintage magazine, but they were made in hard cotton. I've adapted it for lovely soft 100% wool and made these cute slippers a little deeper with a pretty picot edging.

level 2: Improver

materials
Colorway 1
Rooster Baby Rooster (100% fine merino)
1 x 50g ball (137yds/125m) each of:
409 Pistachio (A)
400 Cornish (B)
402 Parma Violet (C)

Colorway 2
Rooster Baby Rooster (100% fine merino)
1 x 50g ball (137yds/125m) each of:
409 Pistachio (A)
405 Ice Gem (B)
400 Cornish (C)

D/3 (3mm) crochet hook

abbreviations
ch chain
dc double crochet
hdc half double
sc single crochet
ss slip stitch
st(s) stitch(es)

finished measurement
To fit a baby 0-3 months old

gauge
Gauge is not critical on this project.

method
sole (make two)
Using A, make 11ch.
Round 1: 1hdc in third ch from hook, 1hdc in next 7 sts, 6hdc in last ch. Working on opposite side of ch, 1hdc in next 7 ch, 5hdc in last ch, join with a ss in top first hdc. (26 sts)
Round 2: 1ch, 1hdc in next 8 sts, 2hdc in each of next 5 ch, hdc in next 8 sts, 2hdc in each of next 5 sts, join with a ss in top of first hdc. (36 sts)
Round 3: 1ch, 1hdc in next 8 sts, [2hdc in first st, 1hdc in next st] 5 times, 1hdc in next 8 sts [2hdc in first st, 1hdc) 5 times, join with a ss in top of first hdc. (46 sts)

Upper slipper

Round 1: 1ch. Working in back loop of sts only. 1sc in each st to end, join with a ss into first sc (46 sts). (This forms ridge on outside of sole.)

Round 2: 3ch, 1dc in same st, *skip 2 sts, 3dc in next st; rep from * 14 more times, 1dc in same st as ss of previous round, join with a ss in top of first 3ch. (46 sts–16 groups of dc).

Fasten off. Using B, join in at top of fastened off st.

Round 3: 3ch, 1dc in same st, skip 2 sts, 3dc in next st (top of first group of dc), skip next 2 sts, 3dc in next st, *skip 2 sts, 1dc in next st; rep from * 5 more times, **skip 2 sts, 3dc in next st; rep from ** 5 more times, 1dc in same st as ss of previous round, join with a ss in top of first 3ch.

Fasten off.

Front

Using B and working at toe end with toe facing, join yarn to top of second single dc on right of work.

Row 1: 1ch, 1sc in same st, 1sc in next 3 sts, skip next st, ss in next 2 sts, turn.

Row 2: Skip 2 ss from previous row, 1sc in next 4 sts, skip next st, ss in next 2 sts, turn.

Row 3: Skip 2 ss from previous row, 1sc in each of next 4 sts, ss in next 2 sts, turn.

Row 4: Skip 2 ss from previous row, 1sc in each of next 4 sts, ss in next 2 sts, turn.

Row 5: 1ch, 1sc in each st around bootie, join with a ss in first sc. (32 sts)

Fasten off.

Row 6: Join in C to fastened-off st, *3ch, ss into first ch, skip 1 st; rep from * to end, join with a ss into first st.

Fasten off.

Sew in ends.

chapter 3

Confident crocheting

Camellia Blanket

This is a light, beautiful blanket that will brighten your room at any time of year, but the colors evoke the delicate pinks and pale silver shades of summer.

level 3: Enthusiast

materials
Inner Flowers:
Debbie Bliss Cashmerino worsted/Aran (55% merino wool, 33% microfibre, 12% cashmere)
3 x 50g balls (294yds/270m) each of:
019 Lilac (A)
026 Pink (B)
Debbie Bliss Cashmerino light worsted/DK (55% merino wool, 33% microfibre, 12% cashmere)
3 x 50g balls (360yds/330m) 023 Peach (C)

Leaf:
Debbie Bliss Cashmerino light worsted/DK (55% merino wool, 33% microfibre, 12% cashmere)
5 x 50g balls (600yds/550m) 011 Green (D)

One-color squares:
Debbie Bliss Cashmerino worsted/Aran (55% merino wool, 33% microfibre, 12% cashmere)
32 x 50g balls (3136yds/2880m) 027 Silver Grey (MC)

G/6 (4.5mm) crochet hook

abbreviations
ch chain
ch sp chain space
dc double crochet
sc single crochet
ss slip stitch
st(s) stitch(es)
WS wrong side

finished measurement
Approx. 67 x 49in. (170 x 125cm)

gauge
Gauge is not critical on this project.

method

The blanket is made up of a combination of flower squares and single-color squares. Make a total of 143 squares: 25 x A center flower, 24 x B center flower, 23 x C center flower (72 flower squares), and 71 single-color squares.

flower square

Using A, B, or C, 5ch, join with a ss.

Round 1: *1sc, 1dc, 1sc into ring; rep from * 3 more times. (4 petals)

Round 2: *2ch, from WS ss into base of 2nd sc of next petal (pick up 2 loops); rep from * 3 more times. Slip last stitch into first ss. (4 loops)

Round 3: *4dc into next 2ch sp (at back), ss into same ch sp; rep from * 3 more times.

Fasten off.

Continue working with same color. Work into the back of petals, picking up two loops.

Join yarn at base of highest point of previous round.

Round 4: *3ch, ss into middle of base of the next petal; rep from * 3 more times. Slip last st into joining st.

Round 5: *8dc into next 3ch sp, ss into same 3ch sp; rep from * 3 more times. Slip last st into joining st.

Fasten off.

Change to D. Working into back of petals and picking up two loops as follows, join yarn into middle of base of petal (next 8dc) of previous round.

Round 6: *3ch, ss into middle of base of the next petal; rep from * 3 more times. Slip last st into joining st.

Round 7: *10dc into 3ch sp, ss into same 3ch sp; rep from * 3 more times.

Fasten off.

Change to MC.

Working into stitches at top (not at back), join yarn into top of center dc of one leaf.

Round 8: 4ch (counts as 1dc, 1ch), *3dc into next space between leaves, 1ch, 3dc, 2ch, 3dc into top of 5th dc of next leaf, 1ch; rep from * twice more. 3dc, 1ch into space between next leaves, 1ch, 3dc, 2ch, 2dc into same st as start of round, ss into ch sp made from first 4-ch.

Round 9: 3ch, 2dc into same ch sp, 1ch, 3dc into next ch sp, *1ch, 3dc, 2ch, 3dc into next ch sp, 1ch, 3dc into next ch sp, 1ch, 3dc into next ch sp; rep from * twice more. 1ch, 3dc, 2ch, 3dc into next ch sp, 1ch, ss into top of first 3-ch.

Round 10: 1ch, 1sc in top of next 3 sts, 1sc in next ch sp, 1sc in top of next 3 sts, 1sc in next ch sp, *1sc in top of next 3 sts, 2sc in next ch sp, 1sc in top of next 3 sts, 1sc in next ch sp, 1sc in top of next 3 sts, 1sc in next ch sp, 1sc in top of next 3 sts, 1sc in next ch sp; rep from * twice more. 1sc in top of next 3 sts, 2sc in next ch sp, 1sc in top of next 3 sts, 1sc in next ch sp, ss into first ch.

Fasten off.

One-color squares

Using MC, make 4ch, join with a ss.

Round 1: 5ch (counts as 1dc and 2ch), *3dc into ring, 2ch; rep from * twice more, 2dc, ss into 3rd of 5-ch.

Round 2: Ss into next ch sp, 5ch (counts as 1dc and 2ch), 3dc into same sp, *1ch, [3dc, 2ch, 3dc] into next chain sp; rep from * twice more, 1ch, skip 3 sts, 2dc into same space as 5-ch from previous round, ss into 3rd of 5-ch.

Round 3: Ss into next ch sp, 5ch (counts as 1dc and 2ch), 3dc into same sp, *1ch, skip 3dc, 3dc into next ch sp, 1ch, skip 3dc** [3dc, 2ch, 3dc] into next sp; rep from * twice more and then from * to ** once more, 2dc into same space as 5-ch, ss into 3rd of 5-ch.

Round 4: Ss into next ch sp, 5ch (counts as 1dc and 2ch), 3dc into same sp, *[1ch, skip 3dc; 3dc into next ch sp] twice, 1ch, skip 3dc**, [3dc, 2ch, 3dc] into next ch sp; rep from * twice more and from * to ** once more, 2dc into same space as 5-ch, ss into 3rd of 5-ch.

Round 5: 1ch, 1sc into top of next st, 2sc into next ch sp, 1sc into top of next 3 sts, 1sc into next ch sp, 1sc into top of next 3 sts, 1sc into next ch sp, 1sc into top of next 3 sts, 1sc into next ch sp, 1sc into top of next 3 sts, *2sc into next ch sp, 1sc into top of next 3 sts, 1ch, 1sc into top of next 3 sts, 1ch, 1sc into top of next 3 sts, 1ch, 1sc into top of next 3 sts; rep from * once more. 2sc into next ch sp, 1sc into top of next 3 sts, 1ch, 1sc into top of next 3 sts, 1ch, 1sc into top of next 3 sts, 1ch, 1sc into top of next 2 sts, ss into top of first 3ch.

Fasten off.

to make up

The blanket is 11 squares wide x 13 squares
long, with alternating flower squares and one-
color squares. Place different-colored flowers at
random over the blanket and then join squares
using a sc seam. Make edging around edge of
blanket by making 1sc into each st along each
edge, making 5sc into each of 4 corner stitches.
Fasten off. Sew in ends.

tips

The flower centers are mostly in
worsted/Aran weight, but I've also chosen
a peach and green that only come in light
worsted/DK. This makes no difference to the
size and shape of the blanket, so if you
choose your own palette, a similar mix of
light worsted/DK and worsted/Aran yarn
will work just as well. However, if you
choose to make the blanket with only light
worsted/DK yarn, the measurements will
come up smaller.

Sew in ends after completing each square
to avoid having to do them all at the end.

Roses and Posies Tea Cozy

This is the prettiest tea cozy ever with its colorful crocheted roses, which can be made from small scraps of yarn. It is a very good improver's project; the pattern uses single crochet with simple decreases and the roses are made using doubles and trebles.

level 2: Improver

materials
Rooster Almerino worsted/Aran (50% baby alpaca, 50% merino wool)
1 x 50g ball (103yds/94m) each of:
301 Cornish (A)
302 Sugared Almond (B)
Debbie Bliss Rialto light worsted/DK (100% merino wool)
1 x 50g ball (114.5yds/105m) 10 Green (C)
Scraps of a variety of different color yarn in any thickness for roses. Each rose uses approx. 30ft (9m) of yarn.
J/10 (6mm), F/5 (4mm), and E/4 (3.5mm) crochet hooks
Yarn sewing needle

abbreviations
ch chain
dc double crochet
rep repeat
sc single crochet
sc2tog Insert hook into next st, draw a loop through, insert hook into next st, draw a loop through, pull through all 3 sts.
ss slip stitch
st(s) stitch(es)
tr treble crochet
WS wrong side

finished measurement
To fit a medium-sized tea pot (4-6 cups)

gauge
Gauge is not critical on this project.

method
main cozy (make 2 sides)
Use yarn double throughout by winding main ball into two smaller balls and using two strands together.
Using A and J/10 (6mm) hook, make 29ch.
Row 1: 1sc in second ch from hook, 1sc in each ch to end, turn.
Row 2: 1ch, 1sc in each ch to end.
Rep Row 2 until work measures 2.5in. (6.5cm).
Next row: 1ch, sc2tog, 1sc in each st to last 2 sts, sc2tog. (26 sts)
Next row: 1ch, sc2tog, 1sc in each st to last 2 sts, sc2tog. (24 sts)
Change to B.
Next row: 1ch, sc2tog, 1sc in each st to last 2 sts, sc2tog. (22 sts)
Next row: 1ch, 1sc in each st to end.

Next row: 1ch, 1sc in each st to end.
Next row: 1ch, sc2tog, 1sc in each st to last 2 sts, sc2tog. (20 sts)
Next row: 1ch, 1sc in each st to end.
Next row: 1ch, 1sc in each st to end.
Next row: 1ch, sc2tog, 1sc in each st to last 2 sts, sc2tog. (18 sts)
Next row: 1ch, sc2tog, 1sc in each st to last 2 sts, sc2tog. (16 sts)
Next row: 1ch, sc2tog, 1sc in each st to last 2 sts, sc2tog. (14 sts)
Next row: 1ch, sc2tog, 1sc in each st to last 2 sts, sc2tog. (12 sts)
Next row: 1ch, sc2tog, 1sc in each st to last 2 sts, sc2tog. (10 sts)
Next row: 1ch, sc2tog, 1sc in each st to last 2 sts, sc2tog. (8 sts)
Next row: 1ch, 1sc in each st to end.
Fasten off.

top tab

Using one strand of B and F/5 (4mm) hook, make 5ch, 1sc into second
ch from hook, 1sc in each of next 3 ch to end, 1ch, turn. (4 sts)
Next row: 1sc in each st to end, 1ch, turn. (4 sts)
Continue until work measures approx. 6in. (15cm).
Fasten off.

roses

Make approx. 29 roses in a variety of different colors—enough to cover
each side on the top half of the cozy.
Using F/5 (4mm) or E/4 (3.5mm) hook and a scrap of yarn, make 48ch.
Petals 1–3: Skip 3 ch, 1dc in each of next 2 ch, 2ch, ss in next ch, *3ch,
1dc in each of next 2 ch, 2ch, ss in next ch; rep from * once more. (3 petals)
Petals 4–6: *4ch, 1tr in each of next 4 ch, 3ch, ss in next ch; rep from
* twice more.
Petals 7–9: *4ch, 1tr in each of next 6 ch, 3ch, ss in next ch; rep from
* twice more.
Fasten off.

to make up

With WS facing, pin tea cozy sides together, leaving a gap on each side
for handle and spout; try on tea pot and pin to fit, or pin and sew 1in.
(2.5cm) at bottom of each side, leaving a 4in. (10cm) gap on each side.
Fold tab in half and pin in place to top center of cozy. Sew seams across
the top and down sides.

embroidery and roses

Using C, embroider leaves in chain stitch along the top edge of cream
section on both sides.

Press rose petals flat. Starting with smaller petals, coil petals, keeping base
flat at chain edge, stitching in place as you go,. Sew roses tightly together
on each side at the top of cozy.

tip
Crocheting using the yarn doubled up
makes the fabric thicker and so better
for insulating.

Russian Dolls—Babushkas

These dolls are such fun to make and look really cute decorated with embroidered flowers or little crochet flowers. The stitches are very easy, but because the dolls are small, they can be fiddly and require attention to detail, so I have put them at Enthusiast level—but don't let that put you off.

level 3: Enthusiast

materials
Large doll
Rooster Almerino light worsted/DK (50% baby alpaca, 50% merino wool)
1 x 50g ball (103yds/94m) each of:
214 Damson (A)
201 Cornish (B)
213 Cherry (C)
Debbie Bliss Baby Cashmerino (55% merino wool, 33% microfibre, 12% cashmere)
1 x 50g ball (137yds/125m) 011 Chocolate Brown for eyes and hair
Red embroidery floss for mouth

Medium doll
Rowan Pure Wool light worsted/DK (100% superwash wool)
1 x 50g ball (137yds/125m) 036 Kiss (D)
Rooster Almerino light worsted/DK (50% baby alpaca, 50% merino wool)
1 x 50g ball (103yds/94m) each of:
201 Cornish (E)
207 Gooseberry (F)
210 Custard for hair
Rowan Cashsoft 4 ply (58% extra-fine merino, 33% microfibre, 10% cashmere)
1 x 50g ball (197yds/180m) 433 Cream (G)
Black embroidery floss for eyes
Red embroidery floss for mouth

Small doll
Rooster Almerino light worsted/DK (50% baby alpaca, 50% merino wool)
1 x 50g ball (103yds/94m) each of:
211 Brighton Rock (H)
201 Cornish (I)
208 Ocean (J)
201 Custard for hair

Rowan Cashsoft 4 ply (58% extra-fine merino, 33% microfibre, 10% cashmere)
1 x 50g ball (197yds/180m) 433 Cream (K)
Black embroidery floss for eyes
Red embroidery floss for mouth

Tiny doll
Debbie Bliss Rialto light worsted/DK (100% extra-fine merino wool)
1 x 50g ball (114.5yds/105m) 10 Green (L)
Rooster Almerino light worsted/DK (50% baby alpaca, 50% merino wool)
1 x 50g ball (103yds/94m) 201 Cornish (M)
Rowan Pure Wool light worsted/DK (100% superwash wool)
1 x 50g ball (137yds/125m) 036 Kiss (N)
Debbie Bliss Baby Cashmerino (55% merino wool, 33% microfibre, 12% cashmere)
1 x 50g ball (137yds/125m) 011 Chocolate Brown for hair
Rowan Cashsoft 4 ply (58% extra-fine merino, 33% microfibre, 10% cashmere)
1 x 50g ball (197yds/180m) 433 Cream (O)
Black embroidery floss for eyes
Red embroidery floss for mouth

Babushka flowers
Small amount of yarn in each of:
Rooster Almerino light worsted/DK (50% baby alpaca, 50% merino wool)
211 Brighton Rock
210 Custard
207 Gooseberry
203 Strawberry Cream
213 Cherry
Rowan Pure Wool light worsted/DK (100% superwash wool)
036 Kiss

Leaves
Small amount of yarn in:
Debbie Bliss Rialto light worsted/DK (100% extra-fine merino wool)
10 Green
Rooster Almerino light worsted/DK (50% baby alpaca, 50% merino wool)
207 Gooseberry

Fiberfill stuffing
F/5 (4mm), E/4 (3.5mm), and D/3 (3mm) crochet hooks
Yarn sewing needle

abbreviations

beg beginning

ch chain

cont continue

sc single crochet

sc2tog Insert hook into next st, draw a loop through, insert hook into next st, draw a loop through, pull through all 3 sts.

rep repeat

st(s) stitch(es)

special abbreviation

Reverse sc (crab st) Do not turn at end of row. Instead, working from left to right, insert hook in next st to right, yarn over hook, draw yarn through st, yarn over hook, draw yarn through 2 loops on hook.

finished measurements

Large 9in. (22cm) high

Medium 6in. (15cm) high

Small 4½ in. (11cm) high

Tiny 3½in. (9cm) high

gauge

Gauge is not critical on this project.

method

Place st marker at beg of each round.

large doll body

Using F/5 (4mm) hook and A, make 2ch.

Round 1: 6sc into second ch from hook. (6 sts)

Round 2: 2sc in each st. (12 sts)

Round 3: *1sc in next st, 2sc in next st; rep from * to end. (18 sts)

Round 4: *1sc in each of next 2 sts, 2sc in next st; rep from * to end. (24 sts)

Round 5: *1sc in each of next 3 sts, 2sc in next st; rep from * to end. (30 sts)

Round 6: *1sc in each of next 4 sts, 2sc in next st; rep from * to end. (36 sts)

Round 7: *1sc in each of next 5 sts, 2sc in next st; rep from * to end. (42 sts)

Round 8: *1sc in each of next 6 sts, 2sc in next st; rep from * to end. (48 sts)

Rounds 9–13: 1sc in each st. (48 sts)

Change to B.

Round 14: Sc2tog, 1sc in each of next 22 sts, sc2tog, 1sc in each of next 22 sts. (46 sts)

Round 15: 1sc in each st.

Round 16: Sc2tog, 1sc in each of next 21 sts, sc2tog, 1sc in each of next 21 sts. (44 sts)

Round 17: Sc2tog, 1sc in each of next 20 sts, sc2tog, 1sc in each of next 20 sts. (42 sts)

Round 18: 1sc in each st.

Round 19: Sc2tog, 1sc in each of next 19 sts, sc2tog, 1sc in each of next 19 sts. (40 sts)

Round 20: 1sc in each st.

Round 21: Sc2tog, 1sc in each of next 18 sts, sc2tog, 1sc in each of next 18 sts. (38 sts)

Round 22: Sc2tog, 1sc in each of next 17 sts, sc2tog, 1sc in each of next 17 sts. (36 sts)

Round 23: 1sc in each st.

Round 24: Sc2tog, 1sc in each of next 16 sts, sc2tog, 1sc in each of next 16 sts. (34 sts)

Round 25: 1sc in each st. (30 sts)

Round 26: Sc2tog, 1sc in each of next 15 sts, sc2tog, 1sc in each of next 15 sts. (32 sts)

Round 27: Sc2tog, 1sc in each of next 14 sts, sc2tog, 1sc in each of next 14 sts. (30 sts)

Round 28: 1sc in each st.

Round 29: Sc2tog, 1sc in each of next 13 sts, sc2tog, 1sc in each of next 13 sts. (28 sts)

Change to C. Work next round in reverse sc.

Round 30: 1 reverse sc, *make 5ch, 1sc (standard) in second ch from hook, 1sc (standard) in next 4 ch, ss in next st; rep from * once more (headscarf ties). Cont in reverse sc to end. (28 sts)

Stop working in reverse sc and cont in standard sc.

Round 31: 1sc into back of each st in B from Round 29 to end. (28 sts)

Round 32: Sc2tog, 1sc in each of next 12 sts, sc2tog, 1sc in each of next 12 sts. (26 sts)

Rounds 33–34: 1sc in each st. (26 sts)

Round 35: Sc2tog, 1sc in each of next 11 sts, sc2tog, 1sc in each of next 11 sts. (24 sts)

Round 36: Sc2tog, 1sc in each of next 10 sts, sc2tog, 1sc in each of next 10 sts. (22 sts)

Round 37: Sc2tog, 1sc in each of next 9 sts, sc2tog, 1sc in each of next 9 sts. (20 sts)

Round 38: Sc2tog, 1sc in each of next 8 sts, sc2tog, 1sc in each of next 8 sts. (18 sts)

Round 39: Sc2tog, 1sc in each of next 7 sts, sc2tog, 1sc in each of next 7 sts. (16 sts)

Stuff doll.

Round 40: Sc2tog around until hole closes.

Fasten off.

face

Using D/3 (3mm) hook and B, make 2ch.

Round 1: 6sc into second ch from hook. (6 sts)

Round 2: 2sc in each st. (12 sts)

Round 3: *1sc in next st, 2sc in next st; rep from * to end. (18 sts)

Round 4: *1sc in next 2 sts, 2sc in next st; rep from * to end. (24 sts)

Ss into next st and fasten off.

Sew in ends and press face. Using D, embroider two French knots for eyes and embroider mouth. Stitch face onto doll. Follow making-up instructions at end to complete doll.

medium doll body

Using F/5 (4mm) hook and D, make 2ch.

Round 1: 6sc into second ch from hook. (6 sts)

Round 2: 2sc in each st. (12 sts)

Round 3: *1sc in next st, 2sc in next st; rep from * to end. (18 sts)

Round 4: *1sc in each of next 2 sts, 2sc in next st; rep from * to end. (24 sts)

Round 5: *1sc in each of next 3 sts, 2sc in next st; rep from * to end. (30 sts)

Round 6: *1sc in each of next 4 sts, 2sc in next st; rep from * to end. (36 sts)

Rounds 7–8: 1sc in each st. (36 sts)

Change to E.

Rounds 9–11: 1sc in each st. (36 sts)

Round 12: Sc2tog, 1sc in each of next 16 sts, sc2tog, 1sc in each of next 16 sts. (34 sts)

Round 13: Sc2tog, 1sc in each of next 15 sts, sc2tog, 1sc in each of next 15 sts. (32 sts)

Round 14: Sc2tog, 1sc in each of next 14 sts, sc2tog, 1sc in each of next 14 sts. (30 sts)

Round 15: Sc2tog, 1sc in each of next 13 sts, sc2tog, 1sc in each of next 13 sts. (28 sts)

Round 16: Sc2tog, 1sc in each of next 12 sts, sc2tog, 1sc in each of next 12 sts. (26 sts)

Round 17: Sc2tog, 1sc in each of next 11 sts, sc2tog, 1sc in each of next 11 sts. (24 sts)

Round 18: 1sc in each st. (24 sts)

Change to F. Work next round in reverse sc.

Round 19: 1 reverse sc, *make 5ch, 1sc (standard) in second ch from hook, 1sc (standard) in next 4 ch, ss in next st; rep from * once more (headscarf ties). Cont in reverse sc to end. (24 sts)

Stop working in reverse sc and cont in standard sc.

Round 20: 1sc into the back of each st in E from Round 18 to end. (24 sts)

Round 21: Sc2tog, 1sc in each of next 10 sts, sc2tog, 1sc in each of next 10 sts. (22 sts)

Round 22: 1sc in each st. (22 sts)

Round 23: Sc2tog, 1sc in each of next 9 sts, sc2tog, 1sc in each of next 9 sts. (20 sts)

Round 24: Sc2tog, 1sc in each of next 8 sts, sc2tog, 1sc in each of next 8 sts. (18 sts)

Round 25: Sc2tog, 1sc in each of next 7 sts, sc2tog, 1sc in each of next 7 sts. (16 sts)

Stuff doll.

Round 26: Sc2tog around until hole closes.

Fasten off

face

Using D/3 (3mm) hook and G, make 2ch.

Round 1: 6sc into second ch from hook. (6 sts)

Round 2: 2sc in each st. (12 sts)

Round 3: *1sc in next st, 2sc in next st; rep from * to end. (*18 sts*)
Ss into next st and fasten off.

Sew in ends and press face. Using black embroidery floss, embroider two French knots for eyes and using red embroidery floss embroider mouth. Stitch face onto doll. Follow making-up instructions at end to complete doll.

small doll body
Using F/5 (4mm) hook and H, make 2ch.
Round 1: 6sc into second ch from hook. (*6 sts*)
Round 2: 2sc in each st. (*12 sts*)
Round 3: *1sc in next st, 2sc in next st; rep from * to end. (*18 sts*)
Round 4: *1sc in each of next 2 sts, 2sc in next st; rep from * to end. (*24 sts*)
Rounds 5–6: 1sc in each st. (*24 sts*)
Change to I.
Rounds 7–9: 1sc in each st. (*24 sts*)
Round 10: Sc2tog, 1sc in each of next 10 sts, sc2tog, 1sc in each of next 10 sts. (*22 sts*)
Round 11: 1sc in each st. (*22 sts*)
Round 12: Sc2tog, 1sc in each of next 9 sts, sc2tog, 1sc in each of next 9 sts. (*20 sts*)
Round 13: 1sc in each st. (*20 sts*)
Change to J. Work next round in reverse sc.
Round 14: 9 reverse sc, *make 3ch, 1sc (standard) in second ch from hook, 1sc (standard) in next 2ch, ss in next st; rep from * once more (headscarf ties). Cont in reverse sc to end. (*20 sts*)
Stop working in reverse sc and cont in standard sc.
Round 15: 1sc into the back of each st in I from Round 13 to end. (*20 sts*)
Round 16: Sc2tog, 1sc in each of next 8 sts, sc2tog, 1sc in each of next 8 sts. (*18 sts*)
Round 17: Sc2tog, 1sc in each of next 7 sts, sc2tog, 1sc in each of next 7 sts. (*16 sts*)
Round 18: Sc2tog, 1sc in each of next 6 sts, sc2tog, 1sc in each of next 6 sts. (*14 sts*)
Round 19: Sc2tog, 1sc in each of next 5 sts, sc2tog, 1sc in each of next 5 sts. (*12 sts*)
Stuff doll.
Round 20: Sc2tog around until hole closes.
Fasten off.

face
Using D/3 (3mm) hook and K, make 2ch.
Round 1: 6sc into second ch from hook. (*6 sts*)
Round 2: 2sc in each st. (*12 sts*)
Ss into next st and fasten off.

Sew in ends and press face. Using black embroidery floss, embroider two French knots for eyes and using red embroidery floss embroider mouth. Stitch face onto doll. Follow making-up instructions at end to complete doll.

tiny doll body

Using E/4 (3.5mm) hook and L, make 2ch.
Round 1: 6sc into second ch from hook. (6 sts)
Round 2: 2sc in each st. (12 sts)
Round 3: *1sc in next st, 2sc in next st; rep from * to end. (18 sts)
Round 4: 1sc in each st. (18 sts)
Change to M.
Rounds 5–8: 1sc in each st. (18 sts)
Round 9: Sc2tog, 1sc in each of next 7 sts, sc2tog, 1sc in each of next 7 sts. (16 sts)
Round 10: 1sc in each st. (16 sts)
Change to N. Work next round in reverse sc.
Round 11: 9 reverse sc, *make 3ch, 1sc (standard) in second ch from hook, 1sc (standard) in next 2 ch, ss in next st; rep from * once more (headscarf ties). Cont in reverse sc to end. (16 sts)
Stop working in reverse sc and cont in standard sc.
Round 12: 1sc into the back of each stitch in M from Round 10 to end. (16 sts)
Round 13: Sc2tog, 1sc in each of next 6 sts, sc2tog, 1sc in each of next 6 sts. (14 sts)
Stuff doll.
Round 14: Sc2tog, 1sc in each of next 5 sts, sc2tog, 1sc in each of next 4 sts. (12 sts)
Round 15: Sc2tog, 1sc in each of next 4 sts, sc2tog, 1sc in each of next 4 sts. (10 sts)
Round 16: Sc2tog around until hole closes.
Fasten off.

face

Using D/3 (3mm) hook and O, make 2ch.
Round 1: 6sc into second ch from hook. (6 sts)
Round 2: 2sc in each st. (12 sts)
Ss into next st and fasten off.

Sew in ends and press face. Using black embroidery floss, embroider two French knots for eyes and using red embroidery floss embroider mouth. Stitch face onto doll. Follow making-up instructions at end to complete doll.

to make up (all dolls)

Sew headscarf ties in place. Sew hair in place by threading a wool or tapestry needle with hair color and making large stitches from top of doll's head to sides. Embroider flowers and leaves onto doll or sew crochet flowers in place.

crochet flowers

Make several for each doll, each in two colors.
Using size D/3 (3mm) hook and first flower colo,r make 4ch, join with ss to form a ring.
Make 5sc into the ring, join with ss.
Change color.
Ss in first st, *2ch, 1hdc, 2ch, ss in same st, ss into next st; rep from * 4 more times.
Fasten off.

Cherub Dress

Crochet dresses look very cute on little girls. The wool used for this dress has been hand-dyed, but you can use any fingering/4 ply wool. If you'd like a larger size, use light worsted/DK wool and larger hooks.

level 3: Enthusiast

materials
Natural Dye Studio Dazzle fingering/4 ply (100% wool)
2 x 100g hanks (394yds/360m) Mimosa
F/5 (4mm), G/6 (4.5mm), H/8 (5mm), and I/9 (5.5mm) crochet hooks
Yarn sewing needle
1m x ½in. (1cm) wide ribbon
2 x small buttons

abbreviations
beg beginning
ch chain
dc double crochet
dec decrease/decreasing
hdc half doublesc single crochet
rem remaining
RS right side
ss slip stitch
st(s) stich(es)
tr treble crochet

finished measurement
To fit a child 18–24 months old

gauge
20sc x 15 rows over 4in. (10cm) square, using F/5 (4mm) hook.

method
dress bodice
Begin at lower edge of front and back.
Using F/5 (4mm) hook, make 116ch.
Row 1 (RS): 1hdc into third ch from hook, 1hdc in each ch to end, 2ch, turn. (work should now measure approx. 23–24in./58–61cm. Use a smaller size hook if it's too long or a larger size hook if it's too short).

Divide for left front bodice:
Row 1: 1hdc in next st and each of next 23 sts, 2ch, turn.
Row 2: Skip 1 st (counts as 1 dec at armhole edge), 1hdc into next st and into each st to end, 2ch, turn.
Row 3: 1hdc in each st to last 2 sts, skip 1 st, make 1hdc into last st, (makes 1 dec at armhole edge), 2ch, turn.
Row 4: Rep Row 3 (makes 1 dec at front edge).
Row 5: Rep Row 2 (makes 1 dec at front edge).
Rep Rows 4 and 5, dec 1 st at front edge on every row, until 11 sts rem. Work even if necessary until work measures 5in. (12.5cm) above the first row of armhole edging.

Fasten off.

back bodice

Skip 10 sts on first Row 1 for left underarm, join yarn into next st.

Row 1: 2ch, 1hdc into same st as joining st, 1hdc into each of next 45 sts, 2ch, turn.

Row 2: 1hdc into each st across (46 sts), 2ch, turn.

Rep Row 2 until work measures same as left front bodice.

Fasten off.

right front bodice

Skip next 10 sts on first Row 1 for right underarm, join yarn into next st.

Row 1: 2ch, 1hdc into same st as joining st, 1hdc into each rem st, 2ch, turn.

Work as left front bodice, starting at Row 2 and reversing shaping.

Fasten off.

skirt

Turn bodice upside down and work on original chain sts.

Using F/5 (4mm) hook, and with RS facing, join yarn into first ch at beginning of left front 1-ch.

Round 1: 1sc into joining st, 1sc into each ch to last ch of right front, join with a ss into first sc to form a circle. Put marker in loop on hook to mark beg of next round.

Round 2: 5ch, *skip next st, 1tr into next st, 1ch; rep from * to end of round, ss into fourth of first 5ch. (57 spaces)

Round 3: 1ch, 1sc into same st as ss from previous round, *1sc in next ch sp, 1sc into top of tr from previous round; rep from * ending with 1sc in last ch sp, join with ss into first st. (114 sts)

Fasten off.

Divide for back skirt:

Change to G/6 (4.5mm) hook, rejoin yarn in middle of left armhole and

work on next 57 sts (this brings you to middle of right armhole).

Row 1: 2ch, 1sc into each of next 3 sts, *3ch, skip 3 sts, 1sc into next st; rep from * to last 3 sts, 1sc into each st, turn.

Row 2: 2ch, 1hdc into each of next 3 sts, *1hdc, 1dc, 1hdc into 3ch sp; rep from * to last 3 sts, 1hdc into each st, turn.

Row 3: 2ch, 1hdc into next 3 sts, *3ch, skip (1hdc, 1dc, 1hdc), 1sc in next sp; rep from * to last 3 sts, 1hdc into each st, turn.

Row 4: 2ch, 1hdc into next 3 sts *1hdc, 1dc, 1hdc into ch sp; rep from * to last 3 sts, 1hdc into each st, turn.

Row 5: 2ch, 1hdc into next 3 sts *3ch, skip (1hdc, 1dc, 1hdc), 1sc into next sp; rep from * to last 3 sts, 1hdc into each st, turn.

Row 6: 2ch, 1hdc into first st, 2hdc into next st, 1hdc into next st, *1hdc, 1dc, 1hdc into next ch sp; rep from * to last 3 sts, 1hdc into first st, 2hdc into next st, 1hdc into last st, turn.

Row 7: 2ch, 1hdc into next 4 sts, *3ch, skip (1hdc, 1dc, 1hdc), 1sc into next sp; rep from * to last 4 sts, 1hdc into each st, turn.

Row 8: 2ch, 1hdc into next 4 sts, *1hdc, 1dc, 1hdc into next ch sp; rep from * to last 4 sts, 1hdc into each st, turn.

Row 9: 2ch, 1hdc into next 4 sts, *3ch, skip (1hdc, 1dc, 1hdc), 1sc into next sp: rep from * to last 4 sts, 1hdc into each st, turn.

Row 10: 2ch, 1hdc into first st, 2hdc into next st, 1hdc into next 2 sts, *1hdc, 1dc, 1hdc into next ch sp; rep from * to last 4 sts, 1hdc into each of next 2 sts, 2hdc into next st, 1hdc, turn.

Row 11: 1ch, 1sc into next 2 sts, 3ch, skip 2 sts, 1sc into next space, *3ch, 1sc into next sp; rep from * to last 5 sts, 3ch, skip 2 sts, 1sc into next 3 sts, turn.

Change to H/8 (5mm) hook.

Row 12: 2ch, 1hdc into first 3 sts, *1hdc, 1dc, 1hdc into each ch sp; rep from * to last 3 sts, 1hdc into next 3 sts, turn.

Row 13: 1ch, 1sc into next 3 sts, *3ch, 1sc into next sp; rep from * to last 3 sts, 1sc into each st, turn.

Rows 14-17: Rep Rows 12-13 twice more.

Row 18: 2ch, 1hdc into first st, 2hdc into next st, 1hdc into each of next 2 sts, *1hdc, 1dc, 1hdc into each ch sp; rep from * to last 4 sts, 1hdc into each of next 2 sts, 2hdc into next st, 1hdc into last st, turn.

Row 19: 1ch, 1sc into next 3 sts, 3ch, skip 2 sts, 1sc into next st, *3ch, skip next 3 sts, 1sc into next sp; rep from * to last 5 sts, 3ch, skip 2 sts, 1sc into next 3 sts, turn.

Row 20: 2ch, 1hdc into next 3 sts, *1hdc, 1dc, 1hdc into ch sp; rep from * to last 3 sts, 1hdc into last 3 sts, turn.

Row 21: 1ch, 1sc into first 3 sts, *3ch, 1sc into sp; rep from * to last 3 sts, 1sc into last 3 sts, turn.

Rows 22-25: Rep Rows 20-21 twice more.

Row 26: 2ch, 1hdc into next st, 2hdc into next st, 1hdc into next st, *1hdc, 1dc, 1hdc into each ch sp; rep from * to last 3 sts, 1hdc into next st, 2hdc into next st, 1hdc into last st, turn.
Row 27: 1ch, 1sc into next 4 sts, *3ch, 1sc into next sp; rep from * to last 4 sts, 1sc into each st.
Change to I/9 (5.5mm) hook.
Row 28: 2ch, 1hdc into next 4 sts, *1hdc, 1dc, 1hdc into each ch sp; rep from * to last 4 sts, 1hdc into each st.
Row 29: 1ch, 1sc into next 4 sts, *3ch, 1sc into next sp; rep from * to last 4 sts, 1sc into each st.
Rows 30–39: Rep Rows 28–29 five times.
Fasten off.

front skirt
With RS facing, rejoin yarn at right side underarm, using G/6 (4.5mm) hook and work as for back.

to make up
Sew shoulder seams using an overstitch.

armhole edging
Using G/6 (4.5mm) hook, make both armhole edgings the same. With RS facing, join yarn at center of underarm edge.
Round 1: Sc around armhole edge, join with a ss into first sc.
Round 2: 1ch, 1sc into same st as joining st, 1sc in each of next 2 sts, *3ch, 1sc in last sc made (picot made), 1sc in each of next 3 sts; rep from * around, join with ss into first sc.

Fasten off.

front and neck edging
Work in rows using G/6 (4.5mm) hook. With RS facing, join yarn at bottom center of right front.
Row 1: Sc evenly up front edge, around neck, and down left front edge (do not join).
Fasten off.
With RS facing, join yarn in first st on right front.
Row 2: 1ch, 1sc in joining st, 1sc in each of next 2 sts, *3ch, 1sc in last sc made (picot made), 1sc in each of next 2 sts; rep from * around right front, neck, and down left side.
Fasten off.

Sew button onto left-hand side, corresponding with buttonhole (use the picot edging as button fasteners). Sew side seams together.

bottom edging
Starting with RS facing and at right-hand bottom edge (working upside down), and using I/9 (5.5mm) hook, rejoin yarn into a 3-ch sp. Make 1dc, 5tr, 1dc into each 3ch sp around bottom of front and back edge. Join at end with a ss into top of first dc and fasten off.
Sew in ends.

Mrs Mittens Purse

This little purse will make any small child happy; it has a handy strap that goes around the neck, so it can't be lost, and is perfect for pocket money.

level 3: Enthusiast

materials

Rooster Almerino light worsted/DK (50% baby alpaca, 50% merino wool)
1 x 50g ball (124yds/112.5m) 201 Cornish
G/6 (4.5mm) crochet hook
Pair safety eyes
Fabric for purse lining
Sewing needle and thread
4in. (10cm) zipper
Fiberfill stuffing
Pink and black felt for muzzle
Embroidery floss for face and flower details
Yarn sewing needle

abbreviations

beg beginning
ch chain
rep repeat
RS right side
sc single crochet
st(s) stitches
WS wrong side

finished measurement

Approx. 6in. (15cm) diameter

gauge

Gauge is not critical on this project.

method
back of head

Round 1: Make 2ch, 6sc in second ch from hook. (*6 sts*)
Place st marker at beg of each round (when counting, loop on hook counts as one st).
Round 2: 2sc in each st. (*12 sts*)
Round 3: *1sc in next st, 2sc in next st; rep from * to end. (*18 sts*)
Round 4: *1sc in next 2 sts, 2sc in next st; rep from * to end. (*24 sts*)
Round 5: *1sc in next 3 sts, 2sc in next st; rep from * to end. (*30 sts*)
Round 6: *1sc in next 4 sts, 2sc in next st; rep from * to end. (*36 sts*)
Round 7: *1sc in next 5 sts, 2sc in next st; rep from * to end. (*42 sts*)
Round 8: *1sc in next 6 sts, 2sc in next st; rep from * to end. (*48 sts*)
Round 9: *1sc in next 7 sts, 2sc in next st; rep from * to end. (*54 sts*)
Round 10: *1sc in next 8 sts, 2sc in next st; rep from * to end. (*60 sts*)
Round 11: *1sc in next 9 sts, 2sc in next st; rep from * to end. (*66 sts*)
Round 12: *1sc in next 10 sts, 2sc in next st; rep from * to end. (*72 sts*)
Round 13: 1sc in each st.
Fasten off with a long tail approx. 6in. (15cm). Sew in ends.

lining

Cut two circles of lining fabric same size as crocheted pieces, plus ⅝in. (1.5cm) extra all around for seam allowance. Insert zipper by sewing either side to WS of lining circles. Turn through, so RS of lining is to inside. Sew lining together in a circle between zipper ends. Sew the two crochet circles RS together, leaving side open for zipper. Turn through and push purse lining inside crochet purse. Sew the open edges of the crochet circles along the zipper to secure.

face

Round 1: Make 2ch, 6sc in second ch from hook. (*6 sts*)
Place st marker at beg of each round (when counting, loop on hook counts as one st).
Round 2: 2sc in each st. (*12 sts*)
Round 3: *1sc, 2sc; rep from * to end. (*18 sts*)
Round 4: *1sc in next 2 sts, 2sc; rep from * to end. (*24 sts*)
Round 5: *1sc in next 3 sts, 2sc; rep from * to end. (*30 sts*)

Rounds 6–7: 1sc in each st (this forms Mrs Mittens' nose).
Round 8: *1sc in next 4 sts, 2sc; rep from * to end. (36 sts)
Round 9: *1sc in next 5 sts, 2sc; rep from * to end. (42 sts)
Round 10: *1sc in next 6 sts, 2sc: rep from * to end. (48 sts)
Round 11: *1sc in next 7 sts, 2sc: rep from * to end. (54 sts)
Round 12: *1sc in next 8 sts, 2sc: rep from * to end. (60 sts)
Round 13: *1sc in next 9 sts, 2sc: rep from * to end. (66 sts)
Rounds 14–15: 1sc in each st.
Fasten off.

to make up

Insert eyes in place and secure. Crochet or sew face section onto front of purse, leaving seam open to allow for stuffing. Stuff lightly, filling nose section. Crochet or sew seam closed.

ears (make 2)

Make 10 ch.
Round 1: 1sc in 2nd st from hook, 1sc in each ch to end. (9 sts)
Round 2: 1 ch, 1sc in each sc.
Rep Row 2 until work forms a square. Fold square in half to form triangle and sc sides together; at top point, make 2sc.
Fasten off. Pin and sew to head.

face detail

Embroider flower above one eye. Cut small felt circle for muzzle and felt triangle for nose. Sew nose to muzzle. Embroider mouth detail and sew muzzle to face. Embroider whiskers.

strap

Make 101ch (or adjust length to suit).
1sc in second ch from hook, 1sc in each ch to end.
Fasten off and sew ends to either side of purse near ears.

Summer Evening Shawl

This is a delightful light shawl, made with a simple diamond chain stitch, and is a great project to try when you have mastered a few skills.

level 3: Enthusiast

materials
Manos del Uruguay Lace (75% baby alpaca, 20% silk, 5% cashmere)
3 x 50g hanks (1320yds/1200m) 6977 Fay
E/4 (3.5mm) crochet hook

abbreviations
beg beginning
ch chain
ch sp chain space
cont continue
sc single crochet
ss slip stitch
st(s) stitch(es)
tr treble crochet

finished measurement
One size, approx. 67 x 27½in. (170 x 70cm)

gauge
Gauge is not critical on this project.

method

Make 202ch.

Row 1: 1sc in second chain from hook, *7ch, skip 3ch, ss in next ch; rep from * to end, make 9ch, turn.

Row 2: *ss in third ch in center of first 7-ch arch, 7ch; rep from * across row ending with ss in third ch of last arch, 2ch, work 1tr in last st, 8ch, turn.

Row 3: Ss in third ch of first 7-ch arch, *7ch, ss in third ch of next arch; rep from * across, 9ch, turn.

Rep Rows 2 and 3 until work measures approx. 64in. (162cm).

Fasten off.

picot edging

Place st marker at beg of each round.

Round 1: Join yarn into any st and place st marker. Work a complete round of sc, making 4sc into each side and finished edge loops and 1sc into each chain of cast-on edge. Work 3sc into each corner st to make the corners square. To join round, make ss into first sc.

Round 2: Work another round of sc, working 1sc into each foundation row st and 3sc into each corner st. Make 2ch, ss into first sc from previous round.

Round 3: Rep Round 2.

Round 4: 6ch, skip next 2 sts, 1sc in next st, *3ch, skip next 2 sts, 1sc in next st; rep from * to end (cont to work 3sc into corner st as previous rows).

Round 5: 1ch, ss in first 3ch sp, *6ch, ss in fourth ch from hook, 2ch, ss in next 3ch sp; rep from * to end.

Fasten off and sew in ends.

Pavlova

This crochet dessert looks so yummy, you'll just want to eat it! You could also use the fruit to trim other items.

level 3: Enthusiast

materials

Rooster Almerino light worsted/DK (50% baby alpaca, 50% merino wool)
1 x 50g ball (124yds/112.5m) each of:
202 Hazelnut (A)
201 Cornish (B)
207 Gooseberry (E)
Rowan Pure Wool light worsted/DK (100% superwash wool)
1 x 50g ball (137yds/125m) 028 Raspberry (C)
Debbie Bliss Rialto light worsted/DK (100% extra-fine merino wool)
1 x 50g ball (114yds/105m) 15 Deep Purple (D)

D/3 (3mm) crochet hook
Yarn sewing needle
Fiberfill stuffing

abbreviations

ch chain
dc double crochet
dec decrease
foll following
hdc half double
rem remaining
RS right side **sc** single crochet
ss slip stitch
st(s) stitch(es)
yo yarn over hook

special abbreviation

cl (cluster) sc into first st, leaving last loop of each st on hook. *5tr into next st, yarn over hook and draw through all loops on hook (1 cluster).

finished measurement

Approx. 5in. (13cm) diameter

gauge

Gauge is not critical on this project.

method

base

Using A, make 4ch, join with ss to form a ring.
Round 1: 12sc into ring, ss into first ch.
Round 2: 1ch, 2sc into same place as 1ch, 2sc into each st of previous round, ss into top of first st. (24 sts)
Round 3: 1ch, 1sc into each st to end, ss into top of first st. (24 sts)
Round 4: 1ch, 2sc into first st, 1sc into next st, *2sc into next st, 1sc into next st; rep from * to end, ss into first st. (36 sts)
Round 5: Rep Round 3. (36 sts)
Round 6: 1ch, 2sc into first st, *1sc into each of next 2 sts, 2sc into next st; rep from * to last 2 sts, 1sc into each st, ss into top of first st. (48 sts)
Round 7: Rep Round 3. (48 sts)
Round 8: 1ch, 2sc into first st, *1sc into each of next 3 sts, 2sc into next st; rep from * to last 3 sts, 1sc into each st, ss into first st. (60 sts)
Round 9: Rep Round 3. (60 sts)
Round 10: 1ch, 2sc into first st, *1sc into each of next 4 sts, 2sc into next st; rep from * to last 4 sts, 1sc into each st, ss into first st. (72 sts)
Round 11: Rep Round 3. (72 sts)
Round 12: 1ch, 2sc into first st, *1sc into each of next 5 sts, 2sc into next st; rep from * to last 5 sts, 1sc into each st, ss into first st. (84 sts)
Round 13: Rep Round 3. (84 sts)

Side edging:
Using A, 1ch.
Round 1: 1sc into each st (working into back loop only) to end, ss into first st. (84 sts)
Round 2: 1ch, sc2tog, *1sc into next 5 sts, sc2tog; rep from * to last 5 sts, 1sc into each st, ss into first st. (72 sts)
Round 3: 1sc into each st, ss into first st. (72 sts)

top

Using A, work Rounds 1–12 from base pattern.
Fasten off.

cream frill

Using B, make 48ch, ss into first ch to form a ring.

Round 1: 1ch, 1sc into each st, ss into first st.

Work the foll two rounds into back loop of each st only.

Round 2: 2ch, 1hdc into same place as 2ch, 2hdc into each sc of previous round, ss into top of first 2-ch.

Round 3: 3ch, 1dc into same place as 3ch, 3dc into each hdc of previous round, ss into top of first 3-ch.

Work into top 2 loops of each st.

Round 4: 1ch, 1sc into same place as 1ch, 1sc in each dc from previous round, ss into first st.

Fasten off.

raspberries (Make 5 in C, 5 in D)

Make 4ch, join with ss to form a ring.

Round 1: 8sc into ring, ss into first st of previous round.

Round 2: 1ch, 2sc into each st, ss into first st. (*16 sts*)

Round 3: 1ch, 1sc into each st, ss into first st.

Round 4: Rep Round 3.

Round 5: 1ch, sc2tog, *sc2tog; rep from * 6 more times, ss into first st.

Roll small amount of stuffing into ball and place inside raspberry.

Round 6: 1sc into each of rem 8 sts, ss into first st. Leave long length of yarn.

Fasten off.

Thread a yarn sewing needle with yarn and thread through all 8 sts, pull tight and secure.

grape center

Using E, make 8ch.

Row 1: 1sc into second ch from hook, 1sc into each of foll 6ch, turn. (7 sts)

Row 2: 1ch, 1cl, 1sc into next st; rep from * once more, turn. (3 clusters)

Row 3: 1ch, 2sc into first st, *1sc into top of cluster, 1sc into next st; rep from * to last st, 2sc into last st.

Row 4: 1ch, 1sc into first st, (1cl into next st, 1sc into next st) 4 times, turn. (4 clusters)

Rep Rows 3 and 4 once more. (5 clusters)

Row 7: 1ch, skip first st, 1sc into each of next 9 sts, turn. (2 sts dec)

Row 8: 1ch, 1sc into first st, *1cl into next st, sc into next st; rep from * to end. (4 clusters)

Rep Rows 7 and 8 once more ending with 3 clusters.

Fasten off.

individual grapes

Using E, make 4ch, skip 3ch, into next ch make 4tr cluster (same as for grape center), pull yarn tight so that cluster forms a smooth dome on RS, make 3ch, ss into base of cluster.

Fasten off.

to make up

With base facing, place top on base and overstitch in place one row below top seam. Sew approx. three-quarters of the way around, place stuffing inside, and complete sewing up. Place cream frill on top of pavlova base and sew in place. Place raspberries on top of cream frill edge, alternating between dark and mid pink. Sew in place. With grape center facing, sew on the six grapes randomly to form a small dome. Place grape dome on center of pavlova and sew in place.

Felted Cherry Brooch

These cherries are very quick and really cute. They are Improver level because they are small and so a little more fiddly, but the stitch is very simple—so once you've mastered crocheting in the round, give them a go. To felt well, they must be made in 100% wool.

level 2: Improver

materials
Cascade 220 light worsted/DK (100% Peruvian wool)
1 x 100g hank (220yds/200m) each of:
8414 Bright Red (A)
0980 Pesto (B)
E/4 (3.5mm) crochet hook
Yarn sewing needle
Small brooch clip

abbreviations
ch chain
hdc half double
sc single crochet
st(s) stitch(es)
ss slip stitch

finished measurement
Approx. 2¾ in. (7cm) width x 3in. (7.5cm) length

gauge
Gauge is not critical on this project.

method
cherries (make two)
Using A, make 2ch.
Round 1: 6sc in second ch from hook.
Round 2: 2sc in each st. (12 sts)
Round 3: 1sc in each st. (12 sts)
Stuff cherry with scraps of red wool.
Round 4: Sc2tog around. (6 sts)
Continue to sc2tog until hole closes.
Fasten off.
Sew in ends.

stalk (make one)
Using B, make 20ch.
Fasten off.

Leaves (make two)
Using B, make 8ch, ss in second ch from hook, 1sc, 1hdc, 1dc, 1hdc, 1sc, ss in last ch.
Working on other side of ch, ss in second ch from hook, 1sc in next st, 1hdc, 1dc, 1hdc, 1sc, ss.
Fasten off.

to make up
Sew one end of stalk to each cherry. Sew leaves to top of stalk. Wash in washing machine on a hot wash, twice. Attach a brooch pin to back of leaves, so that you can't see it from the front.

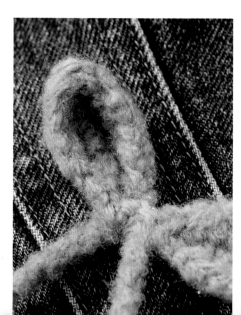

Monty and Priscilla Bear

Although these gorgeous teddies are made using single crochet, which is the most basic stitch, it's in the Enthusiast level because there is a lot of counting during the making. The secret is to count at the end of each round and mark your rounds with a marker; I use a piece of contrasting yarn, or you can buy ready-made stitch markers.

level 3: Enthusiast

materials
teddy 1
Rooster Almerino light worsted/DK (50% baby alpaca, 50% merino wool) 2 x 50g balls (248yds/225m) 205 Glace

teddy 2
Rooster Almerino light worsted/DK (50% baby alpaca, 50% merino wool) 2 x 50g balls (248yds/225m) 203 Strawberry Cream

E/4 (3.5mm) crochet hook
Pair safety eyes
Fiberfill stuffing
Yarn needle
Brown yarn for face details
Ribbon for bow or headband

abbreviations
ch chain
rep repeat
sc single crochet
sc2tog Insert hook into next st, draw a loop through, insert hook into next st, draw a loop through, pull through all 3 sts.
ss slip stitch
st(s) stitch(es)
WS wrong side

finished measurement
Approx. 12in. (31cm) high

gauge
Gauge is not critical on this project.

method
head
Round 1: Make 2ch, 6sc in second ch from hook. (6 sts)
Place st marker at beg of each round. (when counting, loop on hook counts as one st)
Round 2: 2sc in each st. (12 sts)
Round 3: *1sc in first st, 2sc in next st; rep from * to end. (18 sts)
Rounds 4-5: 1sc in each st.
Round 6: *1sc in next 2 sts, 2sc in next sc: rep from * to end. (24 sts)
Rounds 7-8: 1sc in each st. (24 sts)
Round 9: 1sc in next 7 sts, 2sc in next 10 sts, 1sc in next 7 sts. (34 sts)
Round 10: *1sc in next st, 2sc in next st; rep from * once more, 1sc in next 25 sts, 2sc in next st, 1sc in next 2 sts, 2sc in next st, 1sc. (38 sts)
Round 11: 1sc in next 11 sts, 2sc in next st, *1sc in next 2 sts, 2sc in next st; rep from * 4 times more, 1sc in next 11 sts. (44 sts)
Round 12-18: 1sc in each st. (44 sts)
Round 19: 1sc, sc2tog, 1sc in next 2 sts, sc2tog, 1sc in next 30 sts, sc2tog, 1sc in next 2 sts, sc2tog, 1sc. (40 sts)
Round 20: 1sc in next 11 sts, sc2tog, 1sc in next 2 sts, sc2tog, 1sc in next 6 sts, sc2tog, 1sc in next 2 sts, sc2tog, 1sc in next 11 sts. (36 sts)
Round 21: 1sc in each st. (36 sts)
Round 22: *1sc in next 4 sts, sc2tog: rep * to end. (30 sts)
Round 23: *1sc in next 3 sts, sc2tog; rep * to end. (24 sts)
Insert eyes approx. 9 or 10 rows from nose and stuff head.
Round 24: *1sc in next 2 sts, sc2tog; rep * to end. (18 sts)
Round 25: *1sc in next st, sc2tog; rep * to end. (12 sts)
Round 26: Sc2tog around. (6 sts)
Fasten off with a long tail approx. 6in. (15cm). Finish stuffing head, then use yarn needle to thread tail through sts of last round to close gap neatly. Sew in ends.

ears (make 4)
(Do not count loop on hook as one st on this section—st marker is not necessary.)
Make 2ch, 6sc in second ch from hook (do not join ring), turn. (6 sts)
Row 1: 1ch, 1sc in next st, make 2sc in next 4 sts, 1sc. (10 sts)
Row 2: 1ch, 2sc in first st, *1sc in next 2 sts, 2sc in next st; rep from * twice more (14 sts)
Fasten off.

body

Place st marker at beginning of each round.

Round 1: 2ch, 6sc in second ch from hook, join round and each subsequent round with ss. (6 sts)

Round 2: 2sc in each st. (12 sts)

Round 3: *2sc in first st, 1sc in next st; rep from * to end (18 sts)

Round 4: *2sc in first st, 1sc in next 2 sts; rep from * to end. (24 sts)

Rounds 5–7: 1sc in each st. (24 sts)

Round 8: 1sc in first st, 2sc in next st, *1sc in next 3 sts, 2sc in next st; rep from * to last 2 sts, 1sc in each st. (30 sts)

Rounds 9–10: 1sc in each st. (30 sts)

Round 11: *1sc in next 4 sts, 2sc in next st; rep from * to end (36 sts)

Rounds 12–13: 1sc in each st (36 sts)

Round 14: *1sc in next 5 sts, 2sc in next st; rep from * to end (42 sts)

Rounds 15–17: 1sc in each st. (42 sts)

Round 18: 1sc in next 8 sts, 2sc in next st, *1sc in next 4 sts, 2sc in next st; rep from * 4 times more, 1sc in each st to end. (48 sts)

Rounds 19–22: 1sc in each st. (48 sts)

Round 23: 1sc in next 3 sts, sc2tog, *1sc in next 6 sts, sc2tog; rep from * 4 times more, 1sc in each st. (42 sts)

Round 24: 1sc in each st. (42 sts)

Round 25: 1sc in next 4 sts, sc2tog, *1sc in next 9 sts, sc2tog; rep from * twice more, 1sc in next 3 sts. (38 sts)

Round 26: 1sc in next 3 sts, sc2tog, *1sc in next 8 sts, sc2tog, rep from * twice more, 1sc in next 3 sts. (34 sts)

Round 27: 1sc in next 3 sts, sc2tog, *1sc in next 7 sts, sc2tog; rep from * twice more, 1sc in next 2 sts. (30 sts)

Round 28: 1sc in each st. (30 sts)

Round 29: *1sc in next 3 sts, sc2tog; rep from * to end. (24 sts)
Stuff body.

Round 30: *1sc in next 2 sts, sc2tog; rep from * to end. (18 sts)

Round 31: *1sc in next st, sc2tog; rep from * to end. (12 sts)

Round 32: Sc2tog around. (6 sts)

Fasten off with a long tail approx. 6in. (15cm). Finish stuffing body and use yarn needle to thread tail through sts of last round to close gap neatly. Sew in ends.

legs (make two)

Round 1: 2ch, 6sc in second ch from hook.

Round 2: 2sc in each st. (12 sts)

Round 3: *2sc in first st, 1sc in next st; rep from * to end. (18 sts)

Round 4: *2sc in first st, 1sc in next 2 sts; rep from * to end. (24 sts)

Round 5-6: 1sc in each st. (24 sts)

Round 7: *Sc2tog, 1sc in next st; rep from * to end. (16 sts)

Round 8: 1sc in each st. (16 sts)

Rep Round 8 until work measures 4½in. (12cm).
Fasten off. Sew in ends.

arms (make two)

Rep pattern as for legs.
Fasten off. Sew in ends.

to make up

Place two ears with WS together. Join yarn into one corner by pushing hook through both ears. 1ch, make 1sc around by pushing hook through both ears to join top of ears (semi-circle). Ss into bottom corner of semi-circle to join. Rep with other set of ears.
Fasten off. Sew in ends. Sew ears onto head.

Sew body to head, with widest part at bottom. Stuff legs and arms and attach to body. Attach ribbon and tie in a bow around neck or head. Embroider nose and mouth onto face.

tips

Use very soft wool such as Rooster Almerino, which is a mix of alpaca and super-soft merino wool.

Safety eyes are best or embroider the eyes—even if you are not making this for a small child, it may eventually reach little hands or little mouths.

Do not over stuff; teddy should be lovely, soft, and cuddly. When stuffing, break up the fiberfill into small pieces before inserting into toy.

When sewing pieces together, always pin in place first to check that positioning looks correct.

US suppliers

The yarns used in these projects should be available from your local yarn or craft store. If you can't find the correct yarn try some of the companies listed here.

YARN SUPPLIERS

Debbie Bliss
www.debbieblissonline.com

Coats Craft Rowan Yarns
www.coatscrafts.co.uk

Purl Soho
www.purlsoho.com

Yarn Forward
www.yarnforward.com

Fyberspates
www.fyberspates.co.uk

Rooster Yarns
www.laughinghens.com

Rooster & Fyberspates
Knitcellaneous
120 Acorn Street
Merlin,
OR 97532
www.knitcellaneous.com

Bluefaced Leicester
Wool2Dye4
6000-K Boonsboro Road
Coffee Crossing
Lynchburg
VA 24503
www.wool2dye4.com

STOCKISTS

A.C. Moore
Stores nationwide
1-888-226-6673
www.acmoore.com

Crafts, etc.
Online store
1-800-888-0321
www.craftsetc.com

Hobby Lobby
Stores nationwide
www.hobbylobby.com

Jo-Ann Fabric and Craft Store
Stores nationwide
1-888-739-4120
www.joann.com

Knitting Fever
Stockists of Debbie Bliss, Noro, and Sirdar yarns
www.knittingfever.com

Knitting Garden
Stockists of Rowan yarns
www.theknittinggarden.com

Laughing Hens
Wool, patterns, knitting & crochet suppliers
online
www.laughinghens.com

Lets Knit
www.letsknit.com

Michaels
Stores nationwide
1-800-642-4235
www.michaels.com

Unicorn Books and Crafts
www.unicornbooks.com

WEBS
www.yarn.com

Yarn Market
www.yarnmarket.com

UK suppliers

The Berwick Street Cloth Shop
Linings and trimmings
14 Berwick Street
London W1F 0PP
020 7287 2881
www.theberwickstreetclothshop.com

Blue Faced Yarn Shop
H W Hammand & Co
The Croft Stables
Station Lane
Great Barrow
Cheshire CH3 7JN
www.bluefaced.com

Dancing Hens Craft Studio
Wool, books and tuition
Battlers Green Farm
Radlett
Hertfordshire
WD7 8PH
01923 856619
www.dancinghens.com

Debbie Bliss Yarns
Designer Yarns
Units 8-10
Newbridge Industrial Estate
Pitt Street
Keighley
West Yorkshire BD21 4PQ
01535 664222
www.designeryarns.uk.com

Fyberspates
The Maintenance Room
The Nalder Estate
East Challow
Nr Wantage
Oxfordshire
OX12 9SY
07540 656660
www.fyberspates.co.uk

Ingrid Wagner
Giant crochet supplies
Studio 5
The Stone Barn
Kirkharle Courtyard
Kirkharle
Northumberland NE19 2PE
01830 540117
www.ingridwagner.com

John Lewis
Stores nationwide
0845 604 9049
www.johnlewis.com

Natural Dye Studio
Moors Farm
Hollesley
Woodbridge
Suffolk IP12 3RF
01394 411500
www.thenaturaldyestudio.com

Rooster Yarns
Laughing Hens online
Wool, patterns, knitting & crochet supplies
Online.
www.laughinghens.com
01829 740903

Rowan Yarns
Green Lane Mill
Holmfirth
West Yorkshire HD9 2DX
01484 681881
www.knitrowan.com

VV Rouleaux
Ribbons and trimmings
101 Marylebone Lane
London W1U 2QD
020 7224 5179
www.vvrouleaux.com

TUITION

Nicki Trench Workshops
Crochet, knitting, and craft workshops all levels
Email: nicki@nickitrench.com

Index

Acknowledgments

I love crochet and was delighted to be given the opportunity to be involved in a book where I could include all my favourite crochet things. Making this book has been hugely enjoyable on many levels and I'm so lucky to have worked with such an enthusiastic and talented team.

Thank you to all those at Cico, particularly Cindy Richards, Sally Powell and Pete Jorgensen for making my job easy by giving me such a gorgeous palette of colours to work with, beautiful artwork and great organisation. Also big thanks to Marie Clayton for her expert editing eye and crochet knowledge.

I'm indebted to my expert crocheters who helped enormously to get the projects finished in time for the deadlines: Emma Lightfoot, Tracey Elks, Julie Swinhoe, Michelle Bull, Zara Poole and Jenny Shore. Also thanks to Emma Fontaine for her help with the Russian Dolls and Jill Holden for her swift help in pattern checking at the last minute. Also thanks to my many Dancing Hens customers for their invaluable support and sanity checking of the projects. Also to Roger Perkins for coming up with the right words.

I'm also extremely grateful to the UK yarn companies who donated the yarn for the book, particularly to Andy and Johnny at Laughing Hens for the mounds of Rooster yarn; Jenny at Fyberspates, Designer Yarns for Debbie Bliss yarns and to Rowan Yarns for the Amy Butler Belle yarns.

As ever, another huge thanks to my mother, who not only taught me everything I know about crochet but also contributed to making, designing and checking the projects in this book and who I couldn't do without.